Rug Hooking Presents

THE COMPLETE NATURAL DYEING GUIDE

by Marie Sugar

EDITION VI OF RUG HOOKING MAGAZINE'S FRAMEWORK SERIES

EDITOR
Wyatt R. Myers

BOOK DESIGNER
Cher WIlliams

EDITORIAL ASSISTANT
Lisa McMullen

CHAIRMAN
M. David Detweiler

PUBLISHER
J. Richard Noel

Presented by

R·U·G HOOKING

1300 Market St., Suite 202

Lemoyne, PA 17043-1420

(717) 234-5091

(800) 233-9055

www.rughookingonline.com

rughook@paonline.com

 # Acknowledgements

FOR MY FAMILY AND MY HUSBAND, STEVE, FOR HIS ENCOURAGEMENT AND PATIENCE, WHO WROTE THIS POEM FOR ME:

I hear the urgent kitchen sounds
Of clanking pots and pans.
Then smell steamed s̶...
Their way to whi̶...

"Oh, Joy," t̶... ...ut!"
And move with quickened stride.
To see amongst these pots and pans
My friend, my love, my bride.

She sees me near, and says, "Hi, Dear."
And beams a smile quite grand.
Then shows to me no food or tea
But wools dyed in soggy pans.

FOR MY GRANDMOTHER
FOR INSTILLING IN ME THE LOVE OF THE OUTDOORS.

FOR ALL MY FELLOW RUG HOOKERS
WHO CONTRIBUTED IN ONE WAY OR THE OTHER TO
THE WRITING OF THIS BOOK

FOR *RUG HOOKING* MAGAZINE
FOR GIVING ME THE OPPORTUNITY TO EXPRESS MY IDEAS.

—Marie Sugar

Contents

ABOUT THE PUBLISHER

Rug Hooking magazine, the publisher of *The Complete Natural Dyeing Guide*, welcomes you to the rug hooking community. Since 1989 *Rug Hooking* has served thousands of rug hookers around the world with its instructional, illustrated articles on dyeing, designing, color planning, hooking techniques, and more. Each issue of the magazine contains color photographs of beautiful rugs old and new, profiles of teachers, designers, and fellow rug hookers, and announcements of workshops, exhibits, and gatherings.

Rug Hooking has responded to its readers' demand for more inspiration and information by establishing an inviting, informative website at *www.rughookingonline.com* and by publishing a number of books on this fiber art. Along with how-to pattern books and a Sourcebook listing of teachers, guilds, and schools, *Rug Hooking* has produced the competition-based book series *A Celebration of Hand-Hooked Rugs*, now in its 12th year. *The Complete Natural Dyeing Guide* is part of *Rug Hooking*'s popular Framework Series of in-depth educational books.

The hand-hooked rugs you'll see in *The Complete Natural Dyeing Guide* represent just a fragment of the incredible art that is being produced today by women and men of all ages. For more information on rug hooking and *Rug Hooking* magazine, call or write us at the address on page 1.

 # Editor's Note

Before reading Marie Sugar's manuscript, I thought the beautiful flowers, shrubs, and trees around me were a wonderful sight to behold. Beyond that, however, I saw little use for them in my daily life.

Boy was I wrong.

In The Complete Natural Dyeing Guide, *Marie opens up a whole new world of opportunities for these plants. Not only can we enjoy them in nature, but we also can enjoy the beautiful colors they create on our wool. Marie's perspective opened my eyes to a bright new world of color. And whether you're a beginner or an expert,* The Complete Natural Dyeing Guide *will offer you guidance and insight in a comprehensive, accessible book.*

One thing I can say for certain about Marie Sugar is that she is passionate about her dyes. She approaches each trip to the dye pot as a new adventure in color. And each color that emerges from that dye pot—desired or undesired—is an exciting experience. Marie brought both her passion and her expertise as a rug hooking and natural dyeing instructor to the pages of The Complete Natural Dyeing Guide, *and we certainly hope she can instill that same passion in you.*

After designing and color planning, dyeing the wool is often the next crucial step in the rug hooking process. Really, that process of selecting the perfect color for a rug and recreating that color in the dye pot is an art form in and of itself. We felt it was only fitting to devote an entire book to the process of natural dyeing. Like a sheep without its wool, what would your rug be without its vibrant natural colors?

And for many of you Rug Hooking *readers, it is only fitting that I take this moment to introduce myself. I am Wyatt Myers, the new editor of* Rug Hooking *magazine. Though I'm relatively new to the fiber art, I have a strong background as an editor, and I'm looking forward to representing your community through the many books and magazines of* Rug Hooking. *I've already heard from many of you, and I welcome any ideas that you may have. These publications are truly for you and your community, and we at* Rug Hooking *will do our best to make this magazine one that you can be proud of. So without further ado, I present to you our comprehensive guide to the art of natural dyeing. And if you'll excuse me, I have to get back to work on my first rug hooking project. Stay tuned for further updates on how this project is coming along.—Wyatt R. Myers*

Wyatt Myers

An Introduction

I STARTED HOOKING RUGS QUITE BY ACCIDENT. I was a painter and a print-maker before taking up rug hooking. My paintings have been included in many shows and galleries, and my prints are in the permanent collections of the Corcoran Gallery of Art and the National Museum of Women in the Arts, both in Washington, D.C. I also owned an art gallery for some time.

From Painter to Printmaker to Rug Hooker

About five years ago, while I was at a newsstand looking for an art magazine, I spotted *Rug Hooking* magazine. The rug on the front was so beautiful that I was immediately drawn to it. I have been a fan of the needle arts, from cross-stitch to quilting, all my life, so rug hooking naturally intrigued me. When I decided to try it on my own, I was immediately "hooked." (I know you have heard that a million times!) To me, hooking has many similarities to painting. With rug hooking, how-ever, I am using colored wool instead of paint to create my pictures.

For my first rug, I hand-cut each strip with a ruler and a rotary cutter. Then, I hooked the strips very tightly and closely packed together. Needless to say, that first rug buckles a lot!

After that first rug hooking experience, I decided I needed a teacher. I found Roslyn Logsdon teaching at the Montpelier Cultural Arts Center in Laurel, Maryland. Before Roslyn began rug hooking, she was a painter, weaver, and spin-ner, and she shared my idea that rug hooking is as pure an art form as painting.

My first rug used a #5-cut of wool. Since that time, I have tried most cuts of wool: #4, 6, 8, 10, and hand-torn. Many of my rugs fall in the #8- to 10-cut range now, but I skip around to different cuts when I am in the mood. My latest rugs are #8, 10, or hand-torn wool combined with cotton fabrics.

A Little Bit about Me

Before I go on to tell you about my dye recipes, let me share a little of my rug hooking background with you. I have attended the Buckeystown Country Workshops in Maryland, Chincoteaque Rug School in Virginia, the Maryland Shores Rug Hooking School, Roslyn Logsdon's workshops, the Highland School of Rug Hooking in Pennsylvania, as well as a number of smaller workshops. From each class attended and each teacher's influence, I have developed my own style in creating my rug designs. Currently, I am vice-president of the Mason-Dixon Chapter of the Association of Traditional Hooking Artists (ATHA) and have taught a "Rug Design" program for them and for another guild in Maryland. I teach a "Beginning Rug Hooking" class at area fabric stores and art centers. In addition, I have taught natural dyeing in my home studio, and I will teach a natural dyeing course at the Brookfield Craft Center in Connecticut.

Since I am also a beginning weaver, I was a member of a Dye Study Group through the Weavers Guild of Greater Baltimore. Each month, this group explored the use of natural dyes using fibers like wool, cotton, silk, and basketry.

Why I Went Natural

As a result of my painting background, an interest in natural dyeing came naturally to me. As soon as I started rug hooking, I was interested right away in dyeing my wool. When I first began learning about dyeing, I attended workshops where I learned to use synthetic and chemical dyes. While I enjoyed the dyeing process, I soon felt uncomfortable and unsafe working around the chemicals in these dyes. I found it necessary to wear gloves and a mask when handling them because the fumes made me dizzy and sick.

I didn't want to give up dyeing altogether, so I started to think of other ways to dye my wool. My thoughts drifted to the glorious garden of flowers and plants growing in my yard, and I wondered if I could use any of these beautiful plants for natural dyeing.

My curiosity peaked, I started to research the safety of natural dyes. In every book I read, safety issues were still a factor in natural dyeing, but only if the dyer uses certain mordants like tin, chrome, iron, and copper. (A mordant is a chemical that fixes a dye in or on a substance by combining with the dye.) If the mordant alum is used, however, the process of natural dyeing is almost completely safe. Also, I realized that even if a dyer only used alum as the mordant, that person could still create a wide variety of colors.

Soon afterward, a fellow rug hooker, Virginia Pioso, gave me information from her past experiences using natural dyes. My conversations with Virginia made me realize that I could safely create a rainbow of beautiful colors using these dyes. I finally was convinced natural dyeing was safe. Now, I needed to discover if natural dyeing was easy.

Once I decided to further pursue my craft of natural dyeing, I started looking for workshops and classes on the subject. To my surprise, I found very few available. I was lucky that the Weavers Guild scheduled Michele Wipplinger, a natural dye teacher from Seattle, Washington, to give a one-day program here in Maryland. I immediately signed up, and I was very happy to finally find a real person to teach me about natural dyeing. Michele taught me the ease of natural dyeing. Now, I finally felt like I had the tools to get started on my own.

Getting Started with Natural Dyeing

I started the simple way—by using what I already had available in my garden and what I could find in the grocery store. The dye plants growing in my yard were dandelion, rhododendron, sage, pokeweed, grass, tomato vines, acorns, lamb's ear, goldenrod, birch bark, tansy, coreopsis, and marigold. From the grocery store, I tried red and yellow onion skins, blueberries, beets, and carrot tops. My friend, Carolyn, gave me rhubarb leaves from her garden.

Through research, I learned that some plant dyes are more lightfast (resistant to fading from sunlight) than others. They are acorn, birch bark, goldenrod, coreopsis, marigold, and onion skins. Dandelion and carrot tops are not as lightfast, but both are still acceptable dyes that can be overdyed with indigo to make a lightfast green. Experimenting with dyes from each and every plant was a wonderful and enlightening experience.

I do not have a specific garden for growing dye plants. They are scattered throughout my yard and gardens. My dyeing craft has changed one of my habits, however. I have planted marigolds everywhere throughout my yard in order to have enough flowers for dyeing.

A BRIEF HISTORY OF NATURAL DYEING

SINCE THE EARLIEST RECORDED HISTORY OF MANKIND, people have been using natural dyes in one form or another. The cave paintings in Altamira in Spain and Lascaux in France were painted 15,000 years ago with natural dyes and pigments.

In addition, evidence indicates people have been dyeing their cloth using plants and animals for thousands of years. Indigo-dyed cloth from tombs in ancient Thebes dates back to 3,500 B.C. Dyeing was established as a craft in India, China, and South America from about 4,000 to 3,000 B.C. By 1,500 B.C., the Tyrians had perfected a purple dye (Tyrian) obtained from shellfish. They exported the precious purple dye to Rome and other countries. Eight thousand shellfish produced only 1 gram of the precious dye.

In the first century A.D., Egyptian, Indian, and Chinese dyers began using mordants in the dye process. In Europe after 400 A.D., both local and imported dye materials were used.

The dye craft was known in Europe during the Bronze Age and the Iron Age. The Europeans used madder, lichens, weld, and various other dyes. The first dyeing guilds were formed in Germany in Medieval times. In these guilds, master dyers and apprentices took great care to guard their secret dye recipes.

In the 17th century, the East India Trading Company began. For the first time, Europeans were able to trade with India and experience their superior textiles and dyes.

The early dyers in America were trained in Europe, and as a result, they dyed with European ingredients. Soon many rural colonial families began using the plants growing around them for dyeing. We have lost much information on what plants produced which dyes because these early Americans kept few written recipes. Thomas Jefferson and Dolly Madison were in favor of growing dyestuffs in the American colonies so as not to be dependent on foreign supply. Unfortunately, they could not convince the farmers to raise madder, woad, weld, and other dye plants to sell on the commercial market. Cotton and rice were much more profitable to grow. Indigo was cultivated here in early America for about 30 years but soon gave way to cotton and rice. Only since 1856, when a mauve dye made from aniline, a coal-tar, was discovered, have synthetic dyes been available.

STEPHANIE DALTON COWAN

You Don't Need to Garden to Go Natural

You can still use natural dyes even if you don't have a yard or the desire to garden. All the colors you will ever need can be bought from mail-order catalogs. Here is just a sample:

RED: cochineal, madder, brazilwood

BLUE: indigo

YELLOW: fustic, weld

PURPLE: logwood

GREEN: indigo dyed over the yellows

BROWN: cutch

Also, if you are a weaver or a knitter, these dyes can be used on your skeins of wool, silk, and other fibers.

To sum up, why do I use natural dyes? I definitely use them because they are safer than chemical or synthetic dyes. But I also use natural dyes because of my grandmother, who was a great gardener.

Some of my happiest times as a child were spent with her in her garden. My love of gardening came from her gentle guidance in all things growing.

As the years passed, I carried a lot of my childhood memories of my grandmother with me into adulthood. Thanks to her, you can now find me out in the yard in all but a few months of the year. Dyeing with plants is just one more way to enjoy the plants that I care for all year long. I love the fact that some of the colors produced by natural dyes can be bright, but most are softer. Bright or soft, however, they all seem to harmonize well with one another.

One other thing I appreciate about natural dyeing is that it's the dyeing process by which the original hooked rugs were made. By dyeing the wool for my hooked rugs, I really feel like I'm getting in touch with the roots of my craft.

The Test of Time

Our plant kingdom is a virtual rainbow of assorted colors. Almost every plant puts out some sort of color that can be used for dyeing. Natural dyeing has been in use for thousands of years, so some plants and animals have stood the test of time as tried-and-true dye sources. A few of these are indigo, madder, cochineal, logwood, brazilwood, weld, and fustic. In addition, I have included some other plants that also give off a nice-looking dye, although perhaps not quite as nice as the tried-and-true plants.

In the process of writing this book, I experimented with many plants besides the tried-and-true. In the course of my experiments, I've had some disappointing shades come out of the dye pot, and I've had some unexpected, beautiful colors also appear. The surprise that emerges from the dye pot, however, is exactly what is so exciting and fun about natural dyeing. I love opening up the lid on a dye pot the next morning and rinsing the wool to see what beautiful and interesting color has come out.

Included in this book are plants found in your yard, plant nursery, or grocery store, as well as plant extracts you can buy commercially through mail-order catalogs. (For a list of mail-order companies, see page 76.)

In this book, I have put together a good set of dye recipes so you can dye wools a whole range of colors. These colors are lightfast, and they only use alum as a mordant. The hue and intensity of the colors that emerge from your dye pot might be slightly different based on the type of water you have (hard or soft water). Let this book be a starting point for you—please try dyeing with other plants you find interesting.

Before we jump into the dyeing process and the recipes, I have to tell you about one plant you should steer clear of. Though I've been told it makes a wonderful black dye, I don't think any beautiful color is worth dyeing with poison ivy!

The Process of Natural Dyeing

NOW THAT YOU HAVE LEARNED A BIT ABOUT THE HISTORY of natural dyeing and my background with the craft, I bet you're ready to jump right in. Only one problem remains: How do you begin?

First of all, relax! This chapter will make it easy for you to take your fabric from boring to bright in seven easy steps. Then, you'll learn all about the tools you'll need for the natural dyeing process. But first, let's start with the dyeing process, step by step. (Also, be sure to see the sidebars on page 11 for two different processes for dyeing your wool.)

A Step-By-Step Process

Step One: Wash Wool. Use warm to hot water with a little detergent in the washing machine or wash by hand with 1 teaspoon of shampoo.

Step Two: Wet Wool. Soak wool in water overnight with 1 teaspoon of shampoo in order to thoroughly wet the wool.

Step Three: Mordant Wool. For 1 yard of wool, use 2 teaspoons of alum and 1 teaspoon of cream of tartar. Simmer for 1 hour with the lid on. Turn off the heat, and let the wool cool in the pot overnight. Remove the wool, and rinse with water. (*Note: If you want to use more or less wool, increase or decrease the ingredient amounts as it makes sense mathematically. Example: For a $1/2$-yard of wool, use 1 teaspoon of alum and a $1/2$-teaspoon of cream of tartar, etc.*)

Step Four: Simmer Dye Material. Either simmer dye material in a mesh bag in water for 30 to 60 minutes (I use cheesecloth, which can be bought at any grocery or fabric store, for my mesh bag. I also leave the mesh bag in the dye pot while I'm dyeing the wool.)
or
Simmer the powdered dye material in water for 30 minutes. (This step varies from recipe to recipe, and I will tell you which step to use in the specific recipe.)

Step Five: Dye Wool. Add a $1/2$-yard of wet wool to the dye bath, and simmer for 30 to 60 minutes. If you want the color to be darker, leave the wool in longer. (At the end of this 30- to 60-minute step, you can add the "mordant at the end of the dyeing process" that I will discuss in specific recipes.) Turn off the heat, and let the wool cool in the pot overnight. (*Note: If you want to use more or less wool, increase or decrease the dye ingredient amounts as it makes sense mathematically.*)

Step Six: Wash and Rinse. Remove the wool from the dye pot and either wash it in the washing machine on the warm/cool delicate cycle with a little detergent, or wash by hand using 1 teaspoon of shampoo in water. Rinse until the water runs clear.

Step Seven: Hang to Dry. First roll the wet wool in a dry towel to remove excess water. Then hang the wool up to dry or put it in the dryer.

Some Insight into the Dyeing Process.

Dyeing using plants is rather simple. All it really "boils down to" is taking enough of the plant material, containing it in a mesh bag, and heating a large enamel or stainless steel pot of water to a simmer. Then with a lid on, simmer the bag of dye in the water for 30 minutes to 1 hour to release the dye.

Dyeing isn't an exact science, so you may have to add more plants or leave them in the water longer to achieve the depth of color you wish.

THE TOOLS OF THE TRADE

Large Pots: A few basic pieces of equipment are necessary for dyeing, and the most important of these are a few large stainless steel or enamel pots with lids. Before you grab an old pot and start dyeing, however, you should know a few important things. If using an old enamel pot found in a second-hand store, please make sure the pot has no chipped spots. The iron underneath these chipped spots can affect the color in the dye pot.

Smaller Pots: Also helpful for the dyeing process are several other smaller pots. These small pots can be used to transfer the dyed wool out of the big dye pot.

Tongs: A pair of tongs can be useful for grasping the wool and removing it from the hot water.

Rubber Gloves: A pair of heavy-duty rubber gloves can protect your hands from the hot water and keep them from being dyed.

A Mesh Bag: I use cheesecloth, which can be bought at any grocery or fabric store, as the mesh bag to contain the dye material.

A Few Little Things: A few small jars with lids to steep the dye in, measuring spoons, and an apron are the only other tools you'll need for dyeing.

WHEN THE DYE SETS TOO QUICKLY

Sometimes after I put a piece of wool in the dye solution, I achieve the color I want after only 10 minutes or so of dyeing. If this happens, I take out the piece, set it aside, and put in another piece of wool. After I have dyed all the pieces, I put them all back into the pot and simmer them with a lid on for 30 minutes. Then I turn off the heat and leave them to cool in the pot overnight.

With some plants, you may only need 2 cups of flower heads to make a pretty dye. With others, you may need 3 cups. Or you may have to use 3 teaspoons of dye powder instead of two to achieve the color.

How is a dyer supposed to keep track of all of this? I would suggest keeping a record of what you do. (See the dye record on page 12) If the color doesn't come out as you expected, all you have to do is read your record sheet and correct the process next time. Example: Maybe you added 1 cup of flower heads, and the color came out a weak yellow. Next time, add 2 or 3 cups, and see what happens.

If the dye you have ordered comes in powdered form, you usually add 1 to 2 teaspoons to a large pot of water and simmer for 30 minutes. If you used 1 teaspoon of powdered extract and were not satisfied with the depth of color, add 2 teaspoons for a darker shade. If you are using roots or wood chips, soak them in a cup of warm water overnight, and the next day, simmer the bag in a large pot of water for 30 minutes to 1 hour.

Each plant has a particular part that gives off the dye, and this part can vary greatly from plant to plant. The flowers, the leaves, the bark, or the roots all could be the source of the dye. (Each recipe listed in this book includes this information.)

When you're ready to branch out and experiment a bit, you can combine two or more dyes in the same dye pot to create a completely new color. For example, you could stir a $1/2$-teaspoon of lac in the simmering water along with 1 tablespoon of cochineal in a mesh bag. The red shade you produce will be a combination of these two dyes.

At the end of this part of the book, I have included a simple dye record for your information. This record lists the date, dye plant, part of the plant used, the

THE CASSEROLE METHOD

Another way to dye is the casserole method. Rather than a stovetop, the casserole method requires the use of the oven. Instead of simmering, you'll be baking. In the casserole method, feel free to try different flowers and plants for different colors and effects. Follow the steps below to dye using the casserole method.

■ Layer a piece of the wet wool (after you've applied the mordant) in a casserole pan.

■ Sprinkle some of the dyestuff all over the top of the piece of wool. (Red and yellow onion skins or marigold flowers are three dyestuffs that work very well in this manner.)

■ Add another layer of wet wool and sprinkle some more.

■ Repeat until you have layered to the top of the pan.

■ Pour boiling water into the casserole dish until it is halfway filled with water.

■ Cover with foil, and bake in a 300° oven for 30 minutes.

■ Turn off the heat, and let the pan sit in the oven to cool overnight.

■ The next day, hand-wash the wool in water with 1 teaspoon of shampoo, and rinse until the water runs clear.

■ Squeeze out the wet wool, and roll it in a towel to remove the excess water.

■ Hang the wool to dry.

THE SPOT DYE METHOD

Another popular method that you might want to experiment with is spot dyeing. To spot dye your wool, follow the steps below.

■ Use a concentrated form of three separate dyes.

■ To do this, dissolve 1 teaspoon of powdered dye extract in 2 cups of very hot water and stir.

■ Pick out two more colors and do the same. You now have three jars of different colors.

■ Let the dye solutions sit for 30 minutes.

■ Layer a piece of wet wool (after the mordant has been applied) in a large casserole pan.

■ Spoon on the dye separately in spots over the wool.

■ Add another piece of wool and follow the same format.

■ Repeat this process on as many layers as you can until you use up the dye. No need to add more water.

■ Cover with foil and bake at 300° for 30 minutes.

■ Turn the heat off and let the pan sit in the oven to cool overnight.

■ The next day, squeeze out the wool and either put it in the washing machine with a little detergent and wash on the warm, delicate cycle, or hand-wash with 1 teaspoon of shampoo and rinse until the water runs clear. (Note: I have heard that if you add a little fabric softener to the final rinse, the wool is easier to hook.)

■ Hang the wool to dry, or put it in the dryer.

quantity of dye used, amount of fabric used, and the mordant used. At the bottom is a space for notes. I personally use this space to attach a sample of the wool before dyeing and a sample of it after dyeing. Feel free to make as many photocopies of this page as you need. I hope you find it as helpful as I do!

A Few Words about Washing

Having your wool wet before dyeing is a very important and often overlooked step in the dyeing process. To properly wet your wool, submerge it in water with one teaspoon of shampoo and let it soak overnight. The next day, take the wool out of its bath, and rinse it in clear water a few times to remove the shampoo. The wool is now ready to be dyed or have a mordant applied to it.

After the wool has been dyed, you can wash it in two different ways. If you dyed 2 or 3 yards of wool, you might find it much easier to put the wool in the washing machine with a little detergent and run it on the warm/cool delicate cycle. Then hang the wool to

dry, or put it in the dryer.

Personally, I usually hand-wash my dyed wool in warm water with 1 teaspoon of shampoo. Then I rinse the wool until the water comes clear. Afterward, squeeze the water from the wool. Then roll it in a dry towel to remove the excess water, and hang to dry.

As you are washing and rinsing the wool after it has been dyed, you may notice some of the dye coming out. Do not be alarmed, as this is a normal part of the process. Just keep rinsing the wool until the water becomes clear.

Sometimes I like to buy wool garments from thrift shops for my projects. Before dyeing these thrift-shop garments, I throw them in the washing machine with a little detergent using warm to hot water. Then I put them in the dryer. By going through this process first, I remove any dirt, sizing, or dry cleaning chemicals from the fabric. Washing and drying the garment also shrinks the wool.

DYE RECORD

DATE:_____

DYE PLANT:_____

_____

PART OF PLANT USED:_____

_____

QUANTITY USED:_____

AMOUNT OF FABRIC USED:_____

MORDANT:_____

NOTES:_____

_____

_____

_____

_____

_____

_____

_____

_____

_____

_____

_____

_____

_____

_____

_____

_____

_____

_____

_____

Mordants: A Mystery Explained

AS YOU MAY HAVE NOTICED, I HAVE USED THE STRANGE WORD "mordant" several times thus far as I've been explaining the dyeing process. If you're new to dyeing, you're probably wondering by now exactly what a mordant is, and what it's used for. Let me explain. Mordants allow dyes to chemically attach themselves to the wool. They also have an influence on the color itself, and they help keep colors lightfast.

The following is the list of mordants used in natural dyeing. These can be ordered from the suppliers listed in the back of the book.

Mordants

Alum (aluminum potassium sulfate): Alum is the mordant used most by natural dyers, and it's the mordant you will be using in the majority of the dye recipes in this book. A white mineral deposit found around the world, alum is safe to use and found in most kitchen pantries.

While alum is indeed safe to use, you should still be careful how much you add to a dye recipe. If you use more than what the recipe calls for, your wool will come out sticky. I usually put 2 teaspoons in a large pot of water and simmer 1 yard of wool for an hour. I then turn off the heat and let the wool sit in the pot overnight to cool. After rinsing thoroughly, the wool is ready to be dyed.

I also use 1 teaspoon of cream of tartar, which is not a mordant but an assistant, along with alum to soften the wool. Cream of tartar also changes some colors. I only use alum as my mordant and cream of tartar as my assistant for most of my dyeing.

With the remaining four mordants, a level of care must be taken when handling them. They are metallic salts and must be used with caution. As a result of all the beautiful colors I achieve from just using alum, as well as the safety issues involved with the other mordants, I seldom use any other mordant accept alum. (If you're interested in trying a particular mordant, see the list of recipes in each mordant section. These are the dye recipes with which I have had good luck trying that particular mordant.)

Copper (copper sulfate): Also known as blue vitriol, this mordant has a slight greening effect. Copper can be used alone, or it can be added right before you shut off the heat to let the dye pot cool overnight. (Logwood, sandalwood, weld, and sumac are good recipes for trying a copper mordant.)

Tin (stannous chloride): Tin brightens colors, but too much tin makes wool brittle. Tin typically is added at the end of the dyeing process, right before you shut off the heat to let the dye pot cool overnight. (Cochineal, madder, and acorn are good recipes for trying a tin mordant.)

Iron (ferrous sulfate): Also known as copperas, iron saddens or dulls colors. If you use too much, iron will make the wool brittle. Iron is often used at the end of dyeing, right before you shut off the heat to let the dye pot cool overnight. (Black walnut, dyer's broom, yellow dock, acorn, butternut, pomegranate, tea, turmeric, and yarrow are good recipes for trying an iron mordant.)

Chrome (potassium dichromate): Chrome is the most dangerous of all mordants. Use care when dyeing with it by wearing rubber gloves and working in a well-ventilated workspace. Why use chrome if it's so dangerous? People often use chrome for color fastness and to deepen the colors of their fabric. Chrome, however, is very sensitive to light. The dye may be uneven if a lid is not kept on the pot at all times. (Madder and acorn are good recipes for trying a chrome mordant.)

Assistants

Assistants are not mordants, but they do help fabrics absorb the dye and alter the color. I have included a list of assistants in case you might like to experiment with them. (If you're interested in trying a specific assistant, see the list of recipes in each assistant section. These are the dye recipes with which I have had good luck trying that particular assistant.)

Ammonia: After you have completely finished the dyeing process, some dyed fabrics can be soaked in a bath of ammonia (known as an after-bath) to intensify the colors of the fabric. To prepare an ammonia after-bath, simply add 1 cup of ammonia to a separate pot of water. Then soak your fabric in the bath until you achieve the desired color. After soaking the fabric in the bath, proceed with the rinsing and washing procedure listed in each chapter. (Cochineal, copper pennies, indigo, lichens, and woad are good recipes for trying ammonia.)

Baking Soda: An alkali, baking soda also can be used as an after-bath to change colors. After soaking the fabric in the bath, proceed with the rinsing and washing procedure listed in each chapter. (Logwood and sunflower are good recipes for trying baking soda.)

Cream of Tartar: Cream of tartar is primarily used in

the dye bath with alum to keep wool soft and change color.

Glauber's Salt: Glauber's salt slows down the absorption of dyes in the wool, and it prevents streaking of the colors.

Vinegar: Vinegar can alter some colors when used after dyeing as a rinse. After rinsing the fabric with vinegar, proceed with the rinsing and washing procedure listed in each chapter. (Copper pennies and indigo are good recipes for using vinegar.)

Washing Soda: Washing soda is used with some indigo recipes. (See the indigo recipe for more information about washing soda.)

Mordanting as Part of the Dyeing Process

All of these mordants and assistants can be obtained from the "Mail-Order Suppliers" list on page 76, and each one of my recipes gives the specific amount of mordant to be used. All mordants can be used on the wool first before dyeing or added to the dye pot after you shut off the heat to let the wool cool in the dye pot overnight.

The Mordant First/Dye Later Method

For most of my dyeing, I use the method of mordanting first and dyeing later. The benefit of this method is that the mordant remains on the wool longer.

This is the mordanting process that I typically use:

- Bring a large pot of water to a simmer (not a boil).
- Add 2 teaspoons of alum and 1 teaspoon of cream of tartar.
- Add 1 yard of pre-wetted wool, and stir.
- Put a lid on the pot, and simmer the wool for 1 hour.
- Turn off the heat, and let the pot cool overnight.
- Remove the wool from the pot, and rinse in clear warm water a few times.

Now the wool is ready to be dyed. (Note: You can

also mordant with alum first, and then add another mordant at the end of dyeing to change the color of the fabric.)

The One-Pot Method

The second method for mordanting is the one-pot method, and I use this when I am conducting a workshop. The benefit of the one-pot method is that it will save you a step in the process.

The Procedure:

- Bring a large pot of water to a simmer (not a boil).
- Add 2 teaspoons of alum and 1 teaspoon of cream of tartar, and stir.
- Add the dye, and simmer for 30 minutes to 1 hour.
- Add 1 yard of pre-wetted wool, and simmer another 30 minutes to 1 hour.
- Turn off the heat, and let the wool cool in the pot overnight.
- Remove the wool, and wash with 1 teaspoon of shampoo in warm water and rinse until the water runs clear.

Safety Issues

Now that we're just about ready to jump into the dyeing process itself, you should keep in mind a few safety procedures before you start. Please use the following as your safety checklist.

- When using mordants like tin, copper, chrome, or iron, I would suggest putting on rubber gloves, wearing a mask, keeping a lid on the pot, and working in a room with plenty of ventilation. These mordants can be poisonous if used incorrectly. In fact, you should probably wear rubber gloves regardless of the mordant you decide to use. I wear rubber gloves simply because I do not want to burn my hands taking the wool out of the simmering water.
- Label all containers of dye, and store these containers away from children, pets, and food.
- Keep the cooking pots and dyeing pots in separate storage areas.
- Do not use the pots you are dyeing in for cooking.

DYEING DEFINITIONS

Adjective: A dye that requires a mordant to affix the color to the fiber.

Substantive: A dye that requires no mordant to affix the color to the fiber, usually because the dye contains its own mordant. (*Note: Indigo, tea, black walnut, and onion skins are a few dyes that don't need to be mordanted.*)

Mordant: A chemical or mineral salt that binds the dye to the fabric and affects its color and lightfastness.

Assistant: An element used in the dyeing process to alter the final color of the dye.

Lightfastness: The property of a particular dye that rates its resistance to light, especially sunlight.

Fugitive: A dye that will fade over time.

19 Mail-Order Natural Dye Recipes

A T LONG LAST, WE HAVE ARRIVED at the promised dye recipes. In this chapter, I have listed my 19 favorite dye recipes you can create from natural dye sources available through the mail. While this book covers a fair sample of the kinds of dyes you can use, many more are available to the enterprising dyer. In addition, each part of the country has its own special dye plants.

For your convenience, I will repeat the directions in each recipe. You might notice that the directions are similar in most cases.

All the recipes use a $1/2$-yard of pre-wetted, off-white wool. If you want to dye using more or less wool, increase or decrease the dye ingredients as it makes sense mathematically for the specific recipe. You may also dye over any colors, tweeds, or plaids. Most of the recipes use only alum as a mordant, but you can experiment with any of the other mordants to suit your needs.

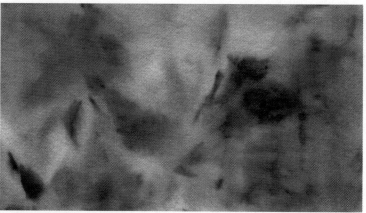

Wool dyed with red and yellow onion skins using the casserole method.

1
Alkanet

(Alkanna tinctoria or Anchusa tinctoria)

- Very good lightfastness
- $5.00/4 oz.
- 1 cup of alkanet (dried roots)
- Mordant used: For a $1/2$-yard of wool, 1 teaspoon of alum and a $1/2$-teaspoon of cream of tartar
- Red and purple shades

Alkanet is a member of the borage family. Various forms of alkanet grow wild in Europe and Britain. The plant can grow to be about 2 feet tall, and it is renowned for its hairy leaves. It has large, blue flowers that bloom in June. The dried roots are the plant part used as the dye.

The Recipe:

1. Put 1 cup of alkanet roots in a mesh bag, and simmer this in a large pot of water for 2 hours with a lid on.
2. Add wet wool, and simmer for 30 minutes.
3. Turn off the heat, and leave the wool in the pot overnight to cool.
4. Remove the wool, and wash in water with 1 teaspoon of shampoo. Rinse until the water runs clear.
5. Squeeze out the wet wool, and roll it in a dry towel to remove the excess water. Hang the wool to dry.
6. Alkanet can be overdyed with indigo to create deep blue or purple shades or overdyed with cutch or black walnut to achieve a purple or brown color.

2
Annatto

(Bixa orellana)

- Very good lightfastness
- $2.00/4 oz.
- 2 tablespoons of annatto seeds
- Mordant used: For a $1/2$-yard of wool, 1 teaspoon of alum and a $1/2$-teaspoon of cream of tartar
- Red and orange shades

Annatto is a shrub native to South and Central America that grows well in all tropical areas. The dye is produced from the seeds. Commonly used during the 18th and 19th centuries, annatto was also used to color butter and cheese.

The Recipe:

1. Crush 2 tablespoons of the seeds and put them in a cheesecloth (mesh) bag.
2. Simmer in a large pot of water for 1 hour with a lid on.
3. Add a $1/2$-yard of wet wool, and simmer for 30 minutes.
4. Turn off the heat, and leave the wool in the pot overnight to cool.
5. Remove the wool, and wash in water with 1 teaspoon of shampoo. Rinse until the water runs clear.
6. Squeeze out the wool, and roll it in a dry towel to remove the excess water. Hang the wool to dry.
7. Annatto can be overdyed with indigo to make a green color. You may want to overdye annatto with lac or madder to achieve deeper orange shades.

3
Black Walnut

(Juglans nigra)

- Excellent lightfastness
- $1.00/4 oz.
- 5 hulls, dried
- No mordant is necessary (Iron + hulls = black or brown shades)
- Brown shades

The black walnut tree is native to North America, and dyeing with black walnuts dates back to the late 1600s. The green hulls are the part of the tree used for dyeing. If you are lucky, you might have a black walnut tree in your yard. For your own use, try to pick up the nuts soon after they fall from the trees. If the nuts lie too long, they start to rot on the ground. Drying the green hulls turns them to a brown color. They can also be frozen for later use.

The Recipe:

1. Soak the 5 hulls in water in a covered container for a couple of days.
2. Pour the water and hulls in a larger pot of water, and heat to a simmer for 1 hour.
3. Put a $1/2$-yard of wet wool in the dye bath, and simmer with the lid on.
4. Keep the wool in as long as necessary to achieve the desired shade, or turn the heat off after 30 minutes to let the wool cool in the pot overnight.
5. Remove the wool, and wash in water with 1 teaspoon of shampoo. Rinse until the water runs clear.
6. Squeeze out the wet wool, and roll it in a dry towel. Hang the wool to dry.
7. If you still have dye in the pot, you can dye more wool. (If you don't want to dye more, the hulls can be taken out and frozen until next time.)
8. A black color can be obtained by dyeing first with black walnut and then overdyeing with indigo.

4
Brazilwood

(Caesalpinia echinata or Haematoxylum brasiletto)

- Very good lightfastness
- $3.00/4 oz.
- 3 tablespoons of brazilwood chips
- Mordant used: For a $1/2$-yard of wool, 1 teaspoon of alum and a $1/2$-teaspoon of cream of tartar
- Rose shades

Brazilwood is obtained from the heartwood of two different redwood trees that are native to India, Malaysia, Ceylon, Nicaragua, Columbia, and Venezuela. This dye was known to Europeans in the 13th century and was an important commercial dyestuff. The wood was also sold for wood chips and sawdust.

The Recipe:

1. Put 3 tablespoons of the brazilwood chips in a mesh bag, and place them in a jar.
2. Pour 1 cup boiling water over them.
3. Leave them to steep overnight.
4. Pour this mixture into a large pot of water and heat to a simmer.
5. Add a $1/2$-yard of wet wool, and simmer for 30 minutes.
6. Turn off the heat, and leave the wool in the pot overnight to cool.
7. Remove the wool, and wash in water with 1 teaspoon of shampoo. Rinse until the water runs clear.
8. Squeeze out the wool, and roll it in a dry towel to remove the excess water. Hang the wool to dry.
9. Brazilwood can be overdyed with madder or lac to create different red shades, or you can put all three in the dye pot at once to achieve various red colors.

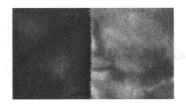

5
Cochineal

(Dactylopius cocus)

- Excellent lightfastness
- $20.00/4 oz.
- 2 tablespoons of dried insects
- Mordant used: For a $1/2$-yard of wool, 1 teaspoon of alum and a $1/2$-teaspoon of cream of tartar
- Rose and red shades

Insects found living on prickly pear cacti in Central and South America, Mexico, and the Canary Islands produce this dye. Cochineal is quite an expensive dye because it takes 70,000 female insects to make 1 pound of dye, but believe me, it's well worth the price. The natives of Mexico were found dyeing with cochineal in 1518 when the Spaniards entered that country. The dried bugs lying on the cactus plants were thought to be seeds, and this is what the Spaniards thought produced the dye. This insect was used to dye the British redcoats their scarlet color.

The Recipe:

1. Soak the insects in a mesh bag in 1 cup of warm water overnight, or crush them into a powder. Then soak the powder in 1 cup of warm water overnight.
2. Pour this concoction into a large pot of water, and simmer with a lid on for one hour. Do not boil!
3. Add a $1/2$-yard of wet wool, and simmer for 30 minutes.
4. Turn off the heat, and leave the wool in the pot overnight to cool.
5. Remove the wool, and wash in water with 1 teaspoon of shampoo. Rinse until the water runs clear.
6. Squeeze out the wool, and roll it in a dry towel to remove the excess water. Hang the wool to dry.
7. When dyeing, you can inject a bit of blue into the dye by adding a $1/2$-cup of ammonia to the dye bath. If tin is added to the dye bath, a scarlet color is obtained. Lac or brazilwood also can be combined with cochineal in the dye bath. Or dye with cochineal, and overdye in another pot with lac or brazilwood.

6
Copper Pennies

- Excellent lightfastness
- 250 pennies
- No mordant is necessary
- Grey shades

Collecting 250 pennies is not as hard as it sounds. You'll be amazed by how many pennies you can find around the house - in drawers, under the sofa cushions, in your coat pockets, or at the bottom of your purse.

The Recipe:

1. Gather about 250 pennies - new or old, it does not matter—and put them in a large pot of water with 1 cup of ammonia added.
2. Add a $1/2$-yard of wet wool, and stir.
3. Put on a tight lid and set the pot out in the garage or in the basement because it's going to smell!
4. Stir the wool twice a day for as many days as you want to achieve the color you desire. The longer the wool is in this solution, the darker it gets. The wool should come out a lovely mottled grey color.
4. Rinse the wool in water with about a cup of vinegar, and then wash with 1 teaspoon of shampoo. Rinse until the water runs clear. The vinegar rinse should remove the ammonia smell from the wool.
5. Squeeze out the wet wool, and roll in a dry towel to remove the excess water. Hang the wool to dry.

7
Cutch

(Acacia catechu or Uncaria gambier)

- Excellent lightfastness
- $4.00/4 oz.
- 2 tablespoons of cutch
- Mordant used: For a $1/2$-yard of wool, 1 teaspoon of alum and a $1/2$-teaspoon of cream of tartar
- Tan and brown shades

Cutch is available as chunks, granules, or a powder. The dye comes from the wood of an acacia tree native to Burma and India.

The Recipe:

1. Pour boiling water over the cutch, and simmer this solution in a large pot of water with a lid on for 30 minutes.
2. Add a $1/2$-yard of wet wool, and simmer for 30 minutes.
3. Turn off the heat, and leave the wool in the pot overnight to cool.
4. Remove the wool, and wash in water with 1 teaspoon of shampoo. Rinse until the water runs clear.
5. Squeeze out the wool, and roll it in a dry towel to remove the excess water. Hang the wool to dry.
6. After you have dyed with cutch, overdye with madder to achieve rust or reddish-brown shades. Overdye with indigo to achieve dark blue or black shades. The wool can also be soaked for several days in the dye bath if you want to achieve deeper shades of tan or brown.

8
Dyer's Broom

(Genista tinctoria)

- Excellent lightfastness
- $8.00/4 oz.
- 6 tablespoons of dried flowers
- Mordant used: For a $1/2$-yard of wool, 1 teaspoon of alum and a $1/2$-teaspoon of cream of tartar.
- Yellow shades

Also called dyer's greenweed, dyer's broom is a hardy perennial. The yellow flowers and green leaves are the parts of the plant that produce the dye. Dyer's broom is found throughout Europe and in parts of North America. The plant has a history of use in dyeing dating back to the 9th century.

The Recipe:

1. Simmer dried flowers and leaves in a mesh bag in a large pot of water for 1 hour with a lid on.
2. Add a $1/2$-yard of wet wool, and simmer for 30 minutes.
3. Turn off the heat, and leave the wool in the pot overnight to cool.
4. Remove the wool, and wash in water with 1 teaspoon of shampoo. Rinse until the water runs clear.
5. Squeeze out the wool, and roll it in a dry towel to remove the excess water. Hang the wool to dry.
6. If you add an iron mordant at the end of dyeing, olive green or brown shades will appear. Dipping the yellow wool in indigo will produce a green color.

9
Fustic

(Chlorophora tinctoria or morus tinctoria)

- Very good lightfastness
- $10.00/4 oz.
- 1 cup of wood chips
- Mordant used: For a $1/2$-yard of wool,
  1 teaspoon of alum and a $1/2$-teaspoon of cream
  of tartar
- Yellow and orange shades

*Also known as old fustic or dyer's mulberry, the dye comes
from the heartwood of a tree that grows in South and
Central America and the West Indies. The tree is a member
of the mulberry family.*

The Recipe:

1. Pour boiling water over the wood chips, which are contained in a mesh bag, and leave it to steep overnight.
2. Pour this concoction into a large pot of water, and simmer for 1 hour with a lid on.
3. Add a $1/2$-yard of wet wool, and simmer for 30 minutes.
4. Turn off the heat, and leave the wool in the pot overnight to cool.
5. Remove the wool, and wash in water with 1 teaspoon of shampoo. Rinse until the water runs clear.
6. Squeeze out the wool, and roll it in a dry towel to remove the excess water. Hang the wool to dry.
7. Overdye the yellow wool with indigo to produce a beautiful green color.

10
Henna

(Lawsonia inermis)

- Very good lightfastness
- $2.00/4 oz.
- 2 teaspoons of powdered henna
- Mordant used: For a $1/2$-yard of wool,
  1 teaspoon of alum and a $1/2$-teaspoon of cream
  of tartar
- Rust shades

*The henna tree is native to Egypt, the Middle East, and
India. Henna is used to dye hair and the body. The leaves
are used as the dye and ground into a powder.*

The Recipe:

1. Simmer henna powder in a large pot of water for 30 minutes with the lid on.
2. Add a $1/2$-yard of wet wool, and simmer for 30 minutes.
3. Turn off the heat, and leave the wool in the pot overnight to cool.
4. Remove the wool, and wash in water with 1 teaspoon of shampoo. Rinse until the water runs clear.
5. Squeeze out the wool, and roll it in a dry towel to remove the excess water. Hang the wool to dry.
6. Henna can be overdyed with any of the red dyes (such as lac, cochineal, and madder, to name a few) to create rusty red colors.

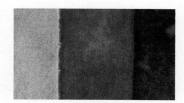

11
Indigo

(Indigofera suffruticosa and Isatis tinctoria,
Indigofera tinctoria, Baptisia tinctoria,
Polygonum tinctorium, Lonchocarpus cyanescens,
Marsdenia species, Nerium tinctorium)

- Very good lightfastness
- Cost varies depending on type of indigo used
  (*see below*).
- Amount varies depending on type of indigo
  used (*see below*).
- No mordant is necessary
- Blue shades

Indigo is a blue dye processed from the leaves of the indigo plant. The plant's dye history is thousands of years old, and it produces an excellent blue dye.

In its earliest times, indigo was grown in India and Egypt. Later, the plant was used by the Romans to make ink. Now the plant is grown all over the world. India brought indigo to Europe in the 16th century. Dutch settlers grew indigo in New York in 1650, and early South Carolina settlers grew indigo from 1740 to 1773. Other colonial states attempted to grow indigo as well, but the crop soon became unprofitable. Indigo was considered the most important dye in America in the 18th and 19th century.

The blue pigment found in indigo is also found in woad (a European herb). Indigo is a perennial shrub in the legume family, and historically, the plant was used as a medicinal source to soothe pain and burns on the skin.

The process for making indigo's blue dye is complicated and time-consuming. It involves placing the indigo leaves in vats with water and soaking them for a few days. The leaves are then removed, and an alkali (like ammonia or urine) is added and stirred into the vat to introduce oxygen. Blue bits of the dye sink to the bottom and form a mud-like sludge. At this point, the liquid part of the dye is drained off, and just the blue sludge is left at the bottom.

The sludge is then removed, dried, and shaped into blocks. At this point, indigo typically is ground into a powder for sale.

Indigo is quite expensive because it takes a large amount of harvested leaves to make a small amount of indigo. Indigo makes a dye of pale blue to very dark blue.

Many recipes for indigo have been passed down through the ages. I have included two here.

To Make an Indigo Vat:

1. Add 1 teaspoon of washing soda (which you can find in the grocery store) to a $1/4$-cup of boiling water, and let it cool.
2. Add 3 teaspoons of indigo powder, and mix into a paste. Let the paste sit for 30 minutes.
3. Bring a large pot of water to a temperature of 120°F. (The water should be hot, but you could still put your hand in it).
4. Add 1 ounce of RIT Color Remover (which you can buy in the grocery store), and stir.
5. After a few minutes, stir in the indigo paste. Take care not to introduce oxygen or air bubbles.
6. The color in the dye pot should change from a blue to a yellow-green after about 45 minutes.
7. To test the color, spoon a little of the dye into a white plastic cup. It should be a yellow-green color. If it is still blue after this time, add a little more RIT Color Remover, and wait until it turns the yellow-green color.
8. Being careful not to add any oxygen, lower your wet wool into the dye bath. No mordant is necessary when dyeing with indigo.
9. Leave the wool in the dye bath for no more than 5 minutes, and remove carefully so that it does not drip back into the vat.
10. As soon as you remove the wool, it should be a green color that quickly will turn to blue.
11. Set the wool aside to air for about 15 minutes.
12. If after this time you wish for a darker shade, dip the wool in the vat again for another 5 minutes.
13. Repeat this process as many times as you wish to achieve the depth of color you desire. If the color in the dye pot turns from the desired yellow-green to blue, sprinkle a little more RIT Color Remover in it, and let it sit awhile until the dye regains its yellow-green color.

14. Remove the wool, and wash in water with 1 teaspoon of shampoo. Rinse until the water runs clear.

15. Squeeze out the wool, and roll it in a dry towel to remove the excess water. Hang the wool to dry.

16. The indigo dye vat can be used over and over. Just add more indigo, and adjust with the RIT Color Remover if necessary.

17. I often overdye the indigo to make green shades. For example, I dye first with indigo, and then I overdye with fustic, weld, marigolds, or any other yellow dye to make green. You also can dip your black walnut-dyed wool in the indigo vat to obtain a blue/black shade.

INSTANT INDIGO

I attended a wonderful natural dye workshop, entitled "Painted Yarn," taught by Michele Wipplinger. She was extremely knowledgeable in the use of natural dyes. "Instant Indigo" is her special indigo recipe. I have used it many times and have consistently produced beautiful shades of blue. This recipe is a quick and easy way to dye with indigo.

The specialty indigo used for this recipe comes from India. It is freeze-dried into crystals in combination with a reducing agent and an alkaline. This form of indigo is concentrated and easy to use. Plus, it is already in its stock form, so the indigo is balanced and ready to use as is.

Instant indigo can be purchased from Michele Wipplinger's company:

EARTHUES,

A NATURAL COLOR COMPANY,

5129 Ballard Avenue N.W.

Seattle, WA 98107

Phone: (206)789-1065

E-mail: earthues@aol.com

PREPARING THE DYE BATH

1 Fill up a large kettle with water, and slowly heat to 120° F or until the water is warm/hot to the touch.

2 Add 2 tablespoons of the dried indigo crystals and stir thoroughly.

3 Check the color of the dye bath. The perfect color should be a green-yellow, clear and bright.

4 In order to see the color change, dribble small amounts of the indigo in a white plastic cup. If the color of the dye bath is yellow, insufficient oxygen is in the water. Whisk or stir the dye bath to create bubbles. The dye bath should then become the green-yellow color.

5 When the dye bath attains the clear green-yellow, you are now ready to dye. (Note: Throughout the entire indigo dyeing process, be sure to hold a constant temperature.)

6 Add the wet wool to the dye bath.

7 Keep the wool in the dye bath anywhere from 2 minutes to a maximum of 10 minutes depending on the depth of shade required, the amount being dyed, and the number of previous dips. Basically, your first dips should only be for 2 to 4 minutes. All other dips can be from 4 minutes up to 10 minutes.

8 Do not squeeze the wool as you remove it from the indigo bath. Just let it drip.

9 The best way to achieve a dark-blue dye from your indigo is to build up the color with a series of successive dips. You cannot dip your wool one time for 1 hour and expect the color to be permanent. Blue colors dyed this way will rub off and wash out constantly. If a light color is desired, it is still best to dip the wool twice, but only for 2 to 3 minutes in a weak dye bath.

12 Remove the wool gently from the dye bath. Try not to add any oxygen by splashing.

13 Set the wool aside for 20 to 30 minutes. The color should change from yellow to green to blue.

14 After 30 minutes, if you want a darker shade, dip the wool another time, and repeat the process. Dip as many times as necessary until the desired shade of blue is achieved. Keep in mind that at least two values of color will be lost to the rinsing and drying process.

15 Add another teaspoon of instant indigo if you notice that the color is not getting any darker after dipping your wool. Wait until the vat achieves the yellow-green color before beginning to dye again.

16 After the last dip, set the wool aside for a day before continuing on with the finishing process.

17 The finishing process includes two steps: neutralizing and washing.

18 Neutralize the wool by soaking it in a pot of warm water with a $1/4$-cup of vinegar added. Soak the wool for 15 minutes.

19 Empty the pot, and wash the wool in very hot water with a little shampoo added for 20 minutes. Often, the wool requires 2 to 3 hot water washings with fresh water to remove excess indigo.

20 End with a series of warm water rinses (no soap) until the color runs clear. Hang the wool to dry.

12
Lac

(resin secreted by scale insects, Coccidae)
- Excellent lightfastness
- $5.00/4 oz.
- 1 teaspoon of lac powder
- Mordant used: For a $1/2$-yard of wool, 1 teaspoon of alum and a $1/2$-teaspoon of cream of tartar
- Mulberry shades

Lac dye comes from the dried resin left behind from insects that feed on ficus trees located in Asia. In India, lac was used for centuries, and Indians introduced the dye to Europe in 1800. You need very little dye powder when dyeing with lac. A little goes a long way!

The Recipe:
1. Simmer lac powder in a large pot of water for 30 minutes with a lid on.
2. Add a $1/2$-yard of wet wool, and simmer for 30 minutes.
3. Turn off the heat, and leave the wool in the pot overnight to cool.
4. Remove the wool, and wash in water with 1 teaspoon of shampoo. Rinse until the water runs clear.
5. Squeeze out the wool, and roll it in a dry towel to remove the excess water. Hang the wool to dry.
6. Lac can be combined with cochineal to produce a scarlet color. Overdye lac with any of the yellows to obtain orange shades.

13
Logwood

(Haematoxylon campechianum)
- Excellent lightfastness
- $10.00/4 oz.
- A $1/2$-teaspoon of powdered logwood
- Mordant used: For a $1/2$-yard of wool, 1 teaspoon of alum and a $1/2$-teaspoon of cream of tartar
- Purple shades

The dye logwood comes from the heartwood of a tree that grows in Central and South America and the West Indies. Logwood comes in powder or wood chip form. The dye was brought to America by English settlers and used in the colonies in the 17th century.

The Recipe:
1. Simmer the powdered logwood in a large pot of water for 15 minutes with a lid on.
2. Add a $1/2$-yard of wet wool, and simmer for 30 minutes.
3. Turn off the heat, and leave the wool in the pot overnight to cool.
4. Remove the wool, and wash in water with 1 teaspoon of shampoo. Rinse until the water runs clear.
5. Squeeze out the wool, and roll it in a dry towel to remove the excess water. Hang the wool to dry.
6. *If using the chips, pour boiling water over 2 tablespoons contained in a mesh bag, and let them sit overnight.
7. *Add this solution to a large pot of water, and simmer for 30 minutes. Continue with the dyeing process. The wood chips can be dried and reused.
8. *After dyeing, rinse the wool in a solution of baking soda and water, and the color will change to a dark blue or a violet. A copper mordant will turn the purple color blue.

Alternate dyeing process

14
Madder

(Rubia tinctorium)

- Excellent lightfastness
- $4.00/4 oz.
- A $1/2$-cup of dried madder root
- Mordant used: For a $1/2$-yard of wool, 1 teaspoon of alum and a $1/2$-teaspoon of cream of tartar
- Red shades

Madder is a perennial plant native to the Middle East, Europe, and Asia Minor and is grown in Italy, France, and Holland. The dye was imported to colonial America from Holland and soon became one of the most important dyes in America. Pliny the Elder mentioned madder in the first century A.D., but it has been used since 2000 B.C. The dye is found in the roots of plants that are harvested after they are 2 or 3 years old. They are dried and can be ground into a powder.

The Recipe:

1. Chop up the dried roots, and soak them in a mesh bag in warm water overnight.
2. Add this solution to a large pot of water and simmer for 30 minutes with the lid on. Do not boil!
3. Add a $1/2$-yard of wet wool, and keep the temperature just below a simmer for 30 minutes.
4. Turn off the heat, and leave the wool in the pot overnight to cool.
5. Remove the wool, and wash in water with 1 teaspoon of shampoo. Rinse until the water runs clear.
6. Squeeze out the wool, and roll it in a dry towel to remove the excess water. Hang the wool to dry.
7. If you are using the powdered form of madder, heat slowly to a simmer for 1 hour, and continue with the process.
8. The roots can be dried and reused again. A tin mordant gives an orange-red color, and a chrome mordant gives a garnet red. Madder can be combined with lac to give off a wonderful red color.

15
Osage Orange

(Maclura pomifera)

- Very good lightfastness
- $3.00/4 oz.
- 4 tablespoons of osage orange
- Mordant used: For a $1/2$-yard of wool, 1 teaspoon of alum and a $1/2$-teaspoon of cream of tartar
- Yellow shades

Osage orange comes from a tree that is a member of the mulberry family. It is also known as hedge apple. The tree bears large yellow fruit, but the bark of the tree is where the dye is derived from. The Osage Indians used the tree for making bows. The wood chips of the tree can be dried and used later.

The Recipe:

1. Soak the wood chips in a mesh bag overnight in warm water.
2. Simmer this solution in a large pot of water for 1 hour with a lid on.
3. Add a $1/2$-yard of wet wool, and simmer for 30 minutes.
4. Turn off the heat, and leave the wool in the pot overnight to cool.
5. Remove the wool, and wash in water with 1 teaspoon of shampoo. Rinse until the water runs clear.
6. Squeeze out the wool, and roll it in a dry towel to remove the excess water. Hang the wool to dry.
7. Overdye with indigo to produce a green color. Overdye with any of the reds like madder, lac or brazilwood to create wonderful orange shades.

16
Sandalwood

(Pterocarpus santalinus)

- Very good lightfastness
- $4.00/4 oz.
- 3 tablespoons of sandalwood
- Mordant used: For a $1/2$-yard of wool, 1 teaspoon of alum and a $1/2$-teaspoon of cream of tartar
- Coral and peach shades

Also called Sanderswood or Saunderswood, sandalwood is a small tree that belongs to the pea family and is grown in the East Indies and Sri Lanka. The dye comes in the form of wood chips or powder made from the heartwood of the tree.

The Recipe:

1. Simmer sandalwood in a mesh bag in a large pot of water for 45 minutes with a lid on.
2. Add a $1/2$-yard of wet wool, and simmer for 30 minutes.
3. Turn off the heat, and leave the wool in the pot overnight to cool.
4. Remove the wool, and wash in water with 1 teaspoon of shampoo. Rinse until the water runs clear.
5. Squeeze out the wool, and roll it in a dry towel to remove the excess water. Hang the wool to dry.
6. Use a copper mordant, and the color will turn a brown shade. You can overdye with indigo, madder, lac, or any of the yellow dyes to make an assortment of different colors. Feel free to experiment.

17
Weld

(Reseda luteola)

- Excellent lightfastness
- $4.00/4 oz.
- 1 cup of dried leaves, flowers, and stalks
- Mordant used: For a $1/2$-yard of wool, 1 teaspoon of alum and a $1/2$-teaspoon of cream of tartar
- Bright yellow shades

Also known as dyer's rocket, weld was grown in England and imported into North America in the 18th century. The plant is a hardy annual that grows up to 6 feet. It was a frequently used dye in Roman times.

The Recipe:

1. Put 1 cup of dried weld in a mesh bag, and pour 1 cup of boiling water over it. Let it steep overnight.
2. Pour this solution into a large pot of water, and simmer for 30 minutes with a lid on.
3. Add a $1/2$-yard of wet wool, and simmer for 30 minutes.
4. Turn off the heat, and leave the wool in the pot overnight to cool.
5. Remove the wool, and wash in water with 1 teaspoon of shampoo. Rinse until the water runs clear.
6. Squeeze out the wool, and roll it in a dry towel to remove the excess water. Hang the wool to dry.
7. Olive green or yellow shades can be achieved with the addition of a copper mordant. Overdye with indigo to create a green color.

check to make sure the color is yellow. If the dye bath is blue, add a $1/2$-teaspoon of RIT Color Remover, and reheat. If the dye bath is greenish-yellow, add 1 teaspoon of ammonia to return the dye bath to the yellow color.

18
Woad

(Isatis tinctoria)

- Very good lightfastness
- $5.00/4 oz.
- 4 cups of dried stem pieces
- No mordant is necessary
- Blue shades

Woad is a biennial. It produces a blue dye, but woad is not as lightfast as indigo. Like indigo, woad is processed as a vat dye. It is an old, traditional dye, but indigo has exceeded its popularity for most people.

The Recipe:

1. Simmer woad in a mesh bag in a large pot of water for 30 minutes. Strain and cool the dye bath.
2. Add 1 tablespoon of ammonia to the strained dye bath.
3. Beat the water for 10 minutes to add oxygen. (It should look blue.)
4. Warm the water, and sprinkle 1 teaspoon of sodium hydrosulphite (RIT Color Remover, which you can get in any grocery store) into the pot. Do not stir. Let this stand for 30 minutes.
5. The perfect time to dye the wool is when the dye bath is a yellow color. To test if the dye bath is yellow, put a little dye in a white plastic cup.
6. Lower the wetted wool slowly into the dye bath, and soak for 15 minutes. Do not stir.
7. Remove the wool carefully and let it air. The color on the wool should be blue.
8. Let the wool sit for 15 minutes. If you wish, you then can resoak for a darker blue.
9. When you have finished dyeing, wash the wool in water with 1 teaspoon of shampoo, and rinse until the water runs clear.
10. Squeeze out the wool, and roll it in a dry towel to remove the excess water. Hang the wool to dry.
11. If you wish to dye again using the same dye bath,

19
Yellow Dock

(Rumex crispus)

- Very good lightfastness
- $4.00/4 oz.
- 3 tablespoons of powder
- Mordant used: For a $1/2$-yard of wool, 1 teaspoon of alum and a $1/2$-teaspoon of cream of tartar
- Yellow shades

Also called curled dock, this root is ground up into a powder to make the dye. Yellow dock is a hardy perennial native to Europe and the United States.

The Recipe:

1. Simmer powder in a large pot of water for 30 minutes with a lid on.
2. Add a $1/2$-yard of wet wool, and simmer for 30 minutes.
3. Turn off the heat, and leave the wool in the pot overnight to cool.
4. Remove the wool, and wash in water with 1 teaspoon of shampoo. Rinse until the water runs clear.
5. Squeeze out the wool, and roll it in a dry towel to remove the excess water. Hang the wool to dry.
6. If you add 2 teaspoons of iron to the dye bath at the end of dyeing, the color changes to an olive green. Overdye with indigo to create a different shade of green.

70 Recipes for Your Garden or Grocery Store

AS YOU PROBABLY NOTICED, MOST OF THE RECIPES from the last chapter were for plants most easily obtained from a mail-order supplier. In this chapter, I'll try to hit a little closer to home. The following recipes are all for plants that you can find in your corner grocery story or grow in the garden at home. After all, what would be nicer than finding a source of color for your wool just outside your front door?

Most of the plants listed in this chapter produce a fair to good dye. For some, the lightfastness rating gets better when you overdye them with another color.

The processing procedure for these dyes is almost identical in all cases.

For flowers and leaves:

1. Use a $1/2$-yard of wet wool that has been treated with an alum mordant and cream of tartar assistant.

2. To extract the dye from flowers and leaves, chop up 4 to 6 cups, and soak them in a mesh bag in water overnight.

3. Add water to this solution to fill a large pot, and heat just to a simmer for 1 hour.

4. Add the wet wool, and simmer for 1 hour.

5. Turn off the heat.

6. Now is the time to add an additional mordant to change the color if you wish.

7. Let the wool cool in the pot overnight.

8. Remove the wool, and wash in water with 1 teaspoon of shampoo, and rinse until the water runs clear.

9. Squeeze out the wet wool, and roll in a dry towel to remove excess water. Hang the wool to dry.

10. You may also pick the flowers as they fade and keep them in a pot of water with a lid on until you have enough.

To dye with berries and nuts:

1. Crush up three cups, and put them in a mesh bag.

2. Continue as if dyeing with flowers.

(Note: The use of different mordants in any of these recipes produces different shades of color.)

1

Acorn

(Quercus)

- Fair lightfastness
- 4 cups of crushed acorns
- No mordant is necessary
- Brown and tan shades

Acorns are the nuts of the oak tree. Collect them when they fall to the ground in September. Be sure to leave enough for your neighborhood squirrels.

The Recipe:

1. Use a $1/2$-yard of wet wool. (No mordant is necessary.)

2. To extract the dye from the acorns, crush up 4 cups, and soak in a mesh bag in water overnight.

3. Add water to this solution to fill a large pot and heat just to a simmer for 1 hour.

4. Add the wet wool and simmer for 1 hour. Turn off the heat.

5. Now is the time to add an additional mordant to change the color, if you want to experiment.

6. Let the wool cool in the pot overnight.

7. Remove the wool, and wash in water with 1 teaspoon of shampoo. Rinse until the water runs clear.

8. Squeeze out the wet wool, and roll in a dry towel to remove excess water. Hang the wool to dry.

9. If you add an iron mordant to the dye at the end of the dyeing process, you may end up with a dark brown. For a golden brown shade, try a chrome or a tin mordant.

2

Aster

(Aster frikartii, Aster novi-belgii, Aster nemoralis)

- Fair lightfastness
- 4 cups of flowers
- Mordant used: For a $1/2$-yard of wool, 1 teaspoon of alum and a $1/2$-teaspoon of cream of tartar
- Yellow shades

Asters can be both an annual and a perennial flower, and many domestic and wild varieties of asters exist. Their flowers range from purple to pink to blue colors. Wild asters grow in fields, and both the wild and domestic varieties bloom in September and October. The fresh flowers are used in dyeing. You may also pick the flowers as they fade and keep them in a pot of water with a lid on until you have enough.

The Recipe:

1. Use a $1/2$-yard of wet wool. (An alum mordant should be applied beforehand.)

2. To extract the dye from the flowers, soak 4 cups in a mesh bag in water overnight.

3. Add water to this solution to fill a large pot and heat just to a simmer for 1 hour.

4. Add the wet wool and simmer for 1 hour. Turn off the heat.

5. Let the wool cool in the pot overnight.

6. Remove the wool, and wash in water with 1 teaspoon of shampoo. Rinse until the water runs clear.

7. Squeeze out the wet wool, and roll in a dry towel to remove excess water. Hang the wool to dry.

8. Overdye with indigo to produce green shades. Overdye with any of the reds (cochineal, lac, or madder to name a few) to obtain orange shades.

3
Bachelor's Button

(Centaurea cyanus)

- Fair lightfastness
- 4 cups of flowers
- Mordant used: For a $1/2$-yard of wool, 1 teaspoon of alum and a $1/2$-teaspoon of cream of tartar
- Yellow shades

Also known as cornflower, this perennial has blue flowers and grows up to 2 feet tall. Bachelor's button blooms in the spring. The fresh flowers are used in dyeing. You may also pick the flowers as they fade and keep them in a pot of water with a lid on until you have enough.

The Recipe:

1. Use a $1/2$-yard of wet wool. (An alum mordant should be applied beforehand.)

2. To extract the dye from the flowers, soak 4 cups in a mesh bag in water overnight.

3. Add water to this solution to fill a large pot and heat just to a simmer for 1 hour.

4. Add the wet wool and simmer for 1 hour. Turn off the heat.

5. Let the wool cool in the pot overnight.

6. Remove the wool, and wash in water with 1 teaspoon of shampoo. Rinse until the water runs clear.

7. Squeeze out the wet wool, and roll in a dry towel to remove excess water. Hang the wool to dry.

8. Overdye with indigo to produce green shades. Overdye with any of the reds (cochineal, lac, or madder to name a few) to obtain orange shades.

4
Barberry

(Berberis)

- Fair lightfastness
- 4 cups of berries
- Mordant used: For a $1/2$-yard of wool, 1 teaspoon of alum and a $1/2$-teaspoon of cream of tartar
- Yellow shades

Barberry is an ornamental shrub. Traditionally, it was used in Europe as a source for yellow dye. The berries are the primary source of the dye.

The Recipe:

1. Use a $1/2$-yard of wet wool. (An alum mordant should be applied beforehand.)

2. To extract the dye from the berries, soak 4 cups in a mesh bag in water overnight.

3. Add water to this solution to fill a large pot and heat just to a simmer for 1 hour.

4. Add the wet wool and simmer for 1 hour. Turn off the heat.

5. Let the wool cool in the pot overnight.

6. Remove the wool, and wash in water with 1 teaspoon of shampoo. Rinse until the water runs clear.

7. Squeeze out the wet wool, and roll in a dry towel to remove excess water. Hang the wool to dry.

8. Overdye with indigo to produce green shades. Overdye with any of the reds (cochineal, lac, or madder to name a few) to obtain orange shades.

5
Bedstraw

(Galium boreali)

- Fair lightfastness
- 4 cups of flowers
- Mordant used: For a $1/2$-yard of wool, 1 teaspoon of alum and a $1/2$-teaspoon of cream of tartar
- Pink shades

Also called lady's bedstraw, bedstraw is a member of the madder family (refer to Part Four). The flowers produce lovely pink shades of dye. You may also pick the flowers as they fade and keep them in a pot of water with a lid on until you have enough.

The Recipe:

1. Use a $1/2$-yard of wet wool. (An alum mordant should be applied beforehand.)

2. To extract the dye from the flowers, soak 4 cups in a mesh bag in water overnight.

3. Add water to this solution to fill a large pot and heat just to a simmer for 1 hour.

4. Add the wet wool and simmer for 1 hour. Turn off the heat.

5. Let the wool cool in the pot overnight.

6. Remove the wool, and wash in water with 1 teaspoon of shampoo. Rinse until the water runs clear.

7. Squeeze out the wet wool, and roll in a dry towel to remove excess water. Hang the wool to dry.

8. Overdye with any of the reds (cochineal, lac, or madder to name a few) to obtain darker red shades and to make the dye more lightfast.

6
Beet

(Beta vulgaris)

- Poor lightfastness
- 4 cups of beets
- Mordant used: For a $1/2$-yard of wool, 1 teaspoon of alum and a $1/2$-teaspoon of cream of tartar
- Pink shades

Beets produce a pink/red dye when steeped in hot water. The dye is fugitive, though. (Note: In dyeing, "fugitive" means that the dye will fade with time.)

The Recipe:

1. Use a $1/2$-yard of wet wool. (An alum mordant should be applied beforehand.)

2. To extract the dye from the beets, soak 4 cups in a mesh bag in water overnight.

3. Add water to this solution to fill a large pot and heat just to a simmer for 1 hour.

4. Add the wet wool and simmer for 1 hour. Turn off the heat.

5. Let the wool cool in the pot overnight.

6. Remove the wool, and wash in water with 1 teaspoon of shampoo. Rinse until the water runs clear.

7. Squeeze out the wet wool, and roll in a dry towel to remove excess water. Hang the wool to dry.

8. Overdye with any of the reds (cochineal, lac, or madder to name a few) to obtain darker red shades and to make it more lightfast.

7
Begonia

(Begonia)

- Fair lightfastness
- 4 cups of flowers
- Mordant used: For a $1/2$-yard of wool, 1 teaspoon of alum and a $1/2$-teaspoon of cream of tartar
- A wide variety of dye shades are possible depending on the color flowers you dyed with.

The begonia is a flowering bulb. The flowers can bloom in red, rust, rose, yellow, orange, and apricot shades. The flowers are best used fresh, but you may also pick the flowers as they fade and keep them in a pot of water with a lid on until you have enough.

The Recipe:

1. Use a $1/2$-yard of wet wool. (An alum mordant should be applied beforehand.)
2. To extract the dye from the flowers, soak 4 cups in a mesh bag in water overnight.
3. Add water to this solution to fill a large pot and heat just to a simmer for 1 hour.
4. Add the wet wool and simmer for 1 hour. Turn off the heat.
5. Let the wool cool in the pot overnight.
6. Remove the wool, and wash in water with 1 teaspoon of shampoo. Rinse until the water runs clear.
7. Squeeze out the wet wool, and roll in a dry towel to remove excess water. Hang the wool to dry.

8
Birch

(Betula)

- Fair lightfastness
- 4 cups of finely chopped bark
- Mordant used: For a $1/2$-yard of wool, 1 teaspoon of alum and a $1/2$-teaspoon of cream of tartar
- Yellow shades

This is an ornamental tree that has white, paper-like bark. Only use the bark that has shredded off the tree and fallen to the ground to make the dye. Pulling bark off the tree may kill the tree.

The Recipe:

1. Use a $1/2$-yard of wet wool. (An alum mordant should be applied beforehand.)
2. To extract the dye from the bark, finely chop the bark, and soak 4 cups in a mesh bag in water overnight.
3. Add water to this solution to fill a large pot and heat just to a simmer for 1 hour.
4. Add the wet wool and simmer for 1 hour. Turn off the heat.
5. Let the wool cool in the pot overnight.
6. Remove the wool, and wash in water with 1 teaspoon of shampoo. Rinse until the water runs clear.
7. Squeeze out the wet wool, and roll in a dry towel to remove excess water. Hang the wool to dry.
8. Overdye with indigo to create greens, and overdye with any of the reds (cochineal, lac, or madder to name a few) to make orange shades.

9
Black-Eyed Susan

(Rudbeckia)

- Fair lightfastness
- 4 cups of flowers
- Mordant used: For a $1/2$-yard of wool, 1 teaspoon of alum and a $1/2$-teaspoon of cream of tartar
- Yellow shades

Black-eyed Susan is a perennial that is also known as coneflower. The yellow flowers that can grow up to 3 feet tall provide the dye from this plant. They bloom from July through September. You may also pick the flowers as they fade and keep them in a pot of water with a lid on until you have enough.

The Recipe:

1. Use a $1/2$-yard of wet wool. (An alum mordant should be applied beforehand.)

2. To extract the dye from the flowers, soak 4 cups in a mesh bag in water overnight.

3. Add water to this solution to fill a large pot and heat just to a simmer for 1 hour.

4. Add the wet wool and simmer for 1 hour. Turn off the heat.

5. Let the wool cool in the pot overnight.

6. Remove the wool, and wash in water with 1 teaspoon of shampoo. Rinse until the water runs clear.

7. Squeeze out the wet wool, and roll in a dry towel to remove excess water. Hang the wool to dry.

8. Overdye with indigo to create greens and overdye with any of the reds (cochineal, lac, or madder to name a few) to make orange shades.

10
Burdock

(Artium minus)

- Fair lightfastness
- 4 cups of leaves
- Mordant used: For a $1/2$-yard of wool, 1 teaspoon of alum and a $1/2$-teaspoon of cream of tartar
- Yellow shades

Burdock is a biennial weed. The leaves are used for the dye.

The Recipe:

1. Use a $1/2$-yard of wet wool. (An alum mordant should be applied beforehand.)

2. To extract the dye from the flowers, soak 4 cups in a mesh bag in water overnight.

3. Add water to this solution to fill a large pot and heat just to a simmer for 1 hour.

4. Add the wet wool and simmer for 1 hour. Turn off the heat.

5. Let the wool cool in the pot overnight.

6. Remove the wool, and wash in water with 1 teaspoon of shampoo. Rinse until the water runs clear.

7. Squeeze out the wet wool, and roll in a dry towel to remove excess water. Hang the wool to dry.

8. Overdye with indigo to create greens and overdye with any of the reds (cochineal, lac, or madder to name a few) to make orange shades.

11
Butternut

(Juglans cinerea)

- Fair lightfastness
- 2 cups of hulls
- No mordant is necessary
- Beige shades

Confederate soldiers' uniforms during the American Civil War were dyed with butternut hulls. As a result, the soldiers became known as the "butternuts."

The Recipe:

1. Use $1/2$-yard wet wool. (No mordant is necessary for butternut.)

2. To extract the dye from the hulls, soak 2 cups in a mesh bag in water overnight.

3. Add water to this solution to fill a large pot, and simmer for 1 to 2 hours.

4. Add the wet wool, and simmer for 1 hour. Turn off the heat.

5. Let the wool cool in the pot overnight.

6. Remove the wool, and wash in water with 1 teaspoon of shampoo. Rinse until the water runs clear.

7. Squeeze out the wet wool, and roll in a dry towel to remove excess water. Hang to dry.

8. *If you are using the commercial powder extract of butternut, simmer the powder in a large kettle of water for 30 minutes. Continue with the dyeing process from there.

9. Overdye with indigo to create greens, and overdye with any of the reds (cochineal, lac, or madder to name a few) to make orange shades. I achieved a lovely grey-green color by adding 2 teaspoons of iron to the dye bath and letting it sit overnight.

*Alternate dyeing process

12
Carrot Tops

(leaves)

- Fair lightfastness
- 4 cups of leaves
- Mordant used: For a $1/2$-yard of wool, 1 teaspoon of alum and a $1/2$-teaspoon of cream of tartar
- Yellow shades

Some grocery stores still sell carrots with the tops attached, but more often, I tend to find the tops of the carrots still attached when I shop in natural food stores.

The Recipe:

1. Use a $1/2$-yard of wet wool. (An alum mordant should be applied beforehand.)

2. To extract the dye from the carrot tops, soak 4 cups in a mesh bag in water overnight.

3. Add water to this solution to fill a large pot and heat just to a simmer for 1 hour.

4. Add the wet wool and simmer for 1 hour. Turn off the heat.

5. Let the wool cool in the pot overnight.

6. Remove the wool, and wash in water with 1 teaspoon of shampoo. Rinse until the water runs clear.

7. Squeeze out the wet wool, and roll in a dry towel to remove excess water. Hang the wool to dry.

8. Overdye with indigo to create greens and overdye with any of the reds (cochineal, lac, or madder to name a few) to make orange shades.

13
Chamomile

(Matricaria maritima, Matricaria Chamomilla)

- Fair lightfastness
- 4 cups of flowers and leaves
- Mordant used: For a $1/2$-yard of wool, 1 teaspoon of alum and a $1/2$-teaspoon of cream of tartar
- Yellow shades

You probably have experienced chamomile in a soothing tea form before bedtime, but our use for chamomile here is a little different. Chamomile produces flowers in late June or July. The yellow flowers and green leaves are used for the dye. You may also pick the flowers as they fade and keep them in a pot of water with a lid on until you have enough.

The Recipe:

1. Use a $1/2$-yard of wet wool. (An alum mordant should be applied beforehand.)

2. To extract the dye from the flowers and leaves, soak 4 cups in a mesh bag in water overnight.

3. Add water to this solution to fill a large pot and heat just to a simmer for 1 hour.

4. Add the wet wool and simmer for 1 hour. Turn off the heat.

5. Let the wool cool in the pot overnight.

6. Remove the wool, and wash in water with 1 teaspoon of shampoo. Rinse until the water runs clear.

7. Squeeze out the wet wool, and roll in a dry towel to remove excess water. Hang the wool to dry.

8. Overdye with indigo to create greens, and overdye with any of the reds (cochineal, lac, or madder to name a few) to make orange shades.

14
Clematis

(Clematis)

- Fair lightfastness
- 4 cups of flowers and vines
- Mordant used: For a $1/2$-yard of wool, 1 teaspoon of alum and a $1/2$-teaspoon of cream of tartar
- Yellow-green shades

Clematis is a flowering perennial vine that produces beautiful flowers in shades of white, red, blue, purple, and yellow. The flowers and vines are used for the dye. You may also pick the flowers as they fade and keep them in a pot of water with a lid on until you have enough.

The Recipe:

1. Use a $1/2$-yard of wet wool. (An alum mordant should be applied beforehand.)

2. To extract the dye from the flowers and vines, soak 4 cups in a mesh bag in water overnight.

3. Add water to this solution to fill a large pot and heat just to a simmer for 1 hour.

4. Add the wet wool and simmer for 1 hour. Turn off the heat.

5. Let the wool cool in the pot overnight.

6. Remove the wool, and wash in water with 1 teaspoon of shampoo. Rinse until the water runs clear.

7. Squeeze out the wet wool, and roll in a dry towel to remove excess water. Hang the wool to dry.

8. Overdye with indigo to create greens.

15
Coreopsis

(Coreopsis tinctoria)

- Fair lightfastness
- 4 cups of flowers
- Mordant used: For a $1/2$-yard of wool, 1 teaspoon of alum and a $1/2$-teaspoon of cream of tartar
- Yellow shades

Coreopsis can either be an annual or a perennial. The yellow flowers bloom all summer long. The flowers are the part of the plant used for the dye. You may also pick the flowers as they fade and keep them in a pot of water with a lid on until you have enough.

The Recipe:

1. Use a $1/2$-yard of wet wool. (An alum mordant should be applied beforehand.)

2. To extract the dye from the flowers, soak 4 cups in a mesh bag in water overnight.

3. Add water to this solution to fill a large pot and heat just to a simmer for 1 to 2 hours.

4. Add the wet wool and simmer for 1 hour. Turn off the heat.

5. Let the wool cool in the pot overnight.

6. Remove the wool, and wash in water with 1 teaspoon of shampoo. Rinse until the water runs clear.

7. Squeeze out the wet wool, and roll in a dry towel to remove excess water. Hang the wool to dry.

8. Overdye with indigo to create greens, and overdye with any of the reds (cochineal, lac, or madder to name a few) to create orange shades.

16
Daffodil

(Narcissus)

- Fair lightfastness
- 4 cups of flowers
- Mordant used: For a $1/2$-yard of wool, 1 teaspoon of alum and a $1/2$-teaspoon of cream of tartar
- Yellow shades

Daffodils are bulbous plants that bloom in the spring. Daffodil blossoms bloom in several different colors like salmon, pink, white, and yellow. The bulbs multiply each year to produce more daffodils. If you can't find enough fresh daffodils at once, you may also pick the flowers as they fade and keep them in a pot of water with a lid on until you have enough.

The Recipe:

1. Use a $1/2$-yard of wet wool. (An alum mordant should be applied beforehand.)

2. To extract the dye from the flowers, soak 4 cups in a mesh bag in water overnight.

3. Add water to this solution to fill a large pot and heat just to a simmer for 1 to 2 hours.

4. Add the wet wool and simmer for 1 hour. Turn off the heat.

5. Let the wool cool in the pot overnight.

6. Remove the wool, and wash in water with 1 teaspoon of shampoo. Rinse until the water runs clear.

7. Squeeze out the wet wool, and roll in a dry towel to remove excess water. Hang the wool to dry.

8. Overdye with indigo to create greens, and overdye with any of the reds (cochineal, lac, or madder to name a few) to create orange shades.

17
Dahlia

(Dahlia)

- Fair lightfastness
- 4 cups of flowers
- Mordant used: For a $1/2$-yard of wool, 1 teaspoon of alum and a $1/2$-teaspoon of cream of tartar
- Yellow shades

Dahlias are bulbs that must be dug up each fall and replanted in the spring. They can grow up to 5 feet tall, and the flowers bloom in shades of rust, red, orange, purple, and scarlet. If you can't find enough fresh dahlias at once, you may also pick the flowers as they fade and keep them in a pot of water with a lid on until you have enough.

The Recipe:

1. Use a $1/2$-yard of wet wool. (An alum mordant should be applied beforehand.)
2. To extract the dye from the flowers, soak 4 cups in a mesh bag in water overnight.
3. Add water to this solution to fill a large pot and heat just to a simmer for 1 hour.
4. Add the wet wool and simmer for 1 hour. Turn off the heat.
5. Let the wool cool in the pot overnight.
6. Remove the wool, and wash in water with 1 teaspoon of shampoo. Rinse until the water runs clear.
7. Squeeze out the wet wool, and roll in a dry towel to remove excess water. Hang the wool to dry.
8. Overdye with indigo to create greens, and overdye with any of the reds (cochineal, lac, or madder to name a few) to create orange shades.

18
Daisy

(Chrysanthemum leucanthemum)

- Fair lightfastness
- 4 cups of flowers
- Mordant used: For a $1/2$-yard of wool, 1 teaspoon of alum and a $1/2$-teaspoon of cream of tartar
- Yellow-green shades

These wildflowers are common throughout Canada and the United States. The white flowers are used for the dye. You may also pick the flowers as they fade and keep them in a pot of water with a lid on until you have enough.

The Recipe:

1. Use a $1/2$-yard of wet wool. (An alum mordant should be applied beforehand.)
2. To extract the dye from the flowers, soak 4 cups in a mesh bag in water overnight.
3. Add water to this solution to fill a large pot and heat just to a simmer for 1 to 2 hours.
4. Add the wet wool and simmer for 1 hour. Turn off the heat.
5. Let the wool cool in the pot overnight.
6. Remove the wool, and wash in water with 1 teaspoon of shampoo. Rinse until the water runs clear.
7. Squeeze out the wet wool, and roll in a dry towel to remove excess water. Hang the wool to dry.
8. Overdye with indigo to create greens.

19
Dandelion Flowers

(Taraxacum officinale)

- Fair lightfastness
- 4 cups of flowers
- Mordant used: For a $1/2$-yard of wool,
  1 teaspoon of alum and a $1/2$-teaspoon of cream
  of tartar
- Yellow shades

Here is a way to use those little yellow flowers that some people call weeds! The dandelion plant has been used medicinally and as a food source for centuries. The roots were also once used in place of coffee. They are perennials that grow to 12 inches tall, and their roots can grow down 18 inches into the ground. You have to use fresh flowers, so you have to be ready to dye as soon as you pick them.

The Recipe:

1. Use a $1/2$-yard of wet wool. (An alum mordant should be applied beforehand.)

2. To extract the dye from the flowers, soak 4 cups in a mesh bag in water overnight.

3. Add water to this solution to fill a large pot and heat just to a simmer for 1 hour.

4. Add the wet wool and simmer for 1 hour. Turn off the heat.

5. Let the wool cool in the pot overnight.

6. Remove the wool, and wash in water with 1 teaspoon of shampoo. Rinse until the water runs clear.

7. Squeeze out the wet wool, and roll in a dry towel to remove excess water. Hang the wool to dry.

8. Overdye with indigo to create greens, and overdye with any of the reds (cochineal, lac, or madder to name a few) to create orange shades.

20
Delphinium

(Delphinium)

- Fair lightfastness
- 4 cups of flowers
- Mordant used: For a $1/2$-yard of wool,
  1 teaspoon of alum and a $1/2$-teaspoon of cream
  of tartar
- Yellow shades

A delphinium is a tall garden perennial with a flower spike. Its blossoms can be blue, purple, pink, and white, and these blossoms are the source of its dye. They bloom in summer. You may also pick the flowers as they fade and keep them in a pot of water with a lid on until you have enough.

The Recipe:

1. Use a $1/2$-yard of wet wool. (An alum mordant should be applied beforehand.)

2. To extract the dye from the flowers, soak 4 cups in a mesh bag in water overnight.

3. Add water to this solution to fill a large pot and heat just to a simmer for 1 hour.

4. Add the wet wool and simmer for 1 hour. Turn off the heat.

5. Let the wool cool in the pot overnight.

6. Remove the wool, and wash in water with 1 teaspoon of shampoo. Rinse until the water runs clear.

7. Squeeze out the wet wool, and roll in a dry towel to remove excess water. Hang the wool to dry.

8. Overdye with indigo to create greens, and overdye with any of the reds (cochineal, lac, or madder to name a few) to create orange shades.

21
Elderberry

(Sambucus canadensis)

- Fair lightfastness
- 4 cups of berries
- Mordant used: For a $1/2$-yard of wool,
  1 teaspoon of alum and a $1/2$-teaspoon of cream
  of tartar
- Pink shades

Elderberry is a shrub that has purple berries. The fruit makes excellent wine and jelly and, conveniently enough, also is used as a dye.

The Recipe:

1. Use a $1/2$-yard of wet wool. (An alum mordant should be applied beforehand.)

2. To extract the dye from the berries, soak 4 cups in a mesh bag in water overnight.

3. Add water to this solution to fill a large pot and heat just to a simmer for 1 to 2 hours.

4. Add the wet wool and simmer for 1 hour. Turn off the heat.

5. Let the wool cool in the pot overnight.

6. Remove the wool, and wash in water with 1 teaspoon of shampoo. Rinse until the water runs clear.

7. Squeeze out the wet wool, and roll in a dry towel to remove excess water. Hang the wool to dry.

8. Overdye with any of the reds (cochineal, lac, or madder to name a few) to create deeper red shades.

22
Geranium

(Pelargonium)

- Fair lightfastness
- 4 cups of flowers
- Mordant used: For a $1/2$-yard of wool,
  1 teaspoon of alum and a $1/2$-teaspoon of cream
  of tartar
- Light green shades

Geraniums are a common houseplant and also a garden flower. Collect the faded blooms for dyeing. The leaves are also used in the dye. The flowers bloom in colors of red, rose, pink, and white. You may also pick the flowers as they fade and keep them in a pot of water with a lid on until you have enough.

The Recipe:

1. Use a $1/2$-yard of wet wool. (An alum mordant should be applied beforehand.)

2. To extract the dye from the flowers, soak 4 cups in a mesh bag in water overnight.

3. Add water to this solution to fill a large pot and heat just to a simmer for 1 hour.

4. Add the wet wool and simmer for 1 hour. Turn off the heat.

5. Let the wool cool in the pot overnight.

6. Remove the wool, and wash in water with 1 teaspoon of shampoo. Rinse until the water runs clear.

7. Squeeze out the wet wool, and roll in a dry towel to remove excess water. Hang the wool to dry.

8. Overdye with indigo to create darker greens.

23
Goldenrod

(Solidago species)

- Fair lightfastness
- 4 cups of flowers
- Mordant used: For a $1/2$-yard of wool,
  1 teaspoon of alum and a $1/2$-teaspoon of cream
  of tartar
- Yellow shades

Found in the United States and Canada, these wildflowers bloom in late summer. These perennials that can grow up to 3 feet tall were commonly used in dyes by American colonists. The flowers should be used when freshly picked, thereby giving off the brightest yellow color. You may also pick the flowers as they fade and keep them in a pot of water with a lid on until you have enough. Goldenrod should not be confused with ragweed, which many people are allergic to.

The Recipe:

1. Use a $1/2$-yard of wet wool. (An alum mordant should be applied beforehand.)

2. To extract the dye from the flowers, soak 4 cups in a mesh bag in water overnight.

3. Add water to this solution to fill a large pot and heat just to a simmer for 1 hour.

4. Add the wet wool and simmer for 1 hour. Turn off the heat.

5. Let the wool cool in the pot overnight.

6. Remove the wool, and wash in water with 1 teaspoon of shampoo. Rinse until the water runs clear.

7. Squeeze out the wet wool, and roll in a dry towel to remove excess water. Hang the wool to dry.

8. Overdye with indigo to create greens, and overdye with any of the reds (cochineal, lac, or madder to name a few) to create orange shades.

24
Grass

(Various species)

- Fair lightfastness
- 4 cups of grass
- Mordant used: For a $1/2$-yard of wool,
  1 teaspoon of alum and a $1/2$-teaspoon of cream
  of tartar
- Yellow-green shades

Grass is one dye ingredient you shouldn't have any trouble finding in abundance in your yard. Collect some grass right after it has been mowed. Be sure not to use any grass that has been treated with chemicals.

The Recipe:

1. Use a $1/2$-yard of wet wool. (An alum mordant should be applied beforehand.)

2. To extract the dye from the grass, soak 4 cups in a mesh bag in water overnight.

3. Add water to this solution to fill a large pot and heat just to a simmer for 1 hour.

4. Add the wet wool and simmer for 1 hour. Turn off the heat.

5. Let the wool cool in the pot overnight.

6. Remove the wool, and wash in water with 1 teaspoon of shampoo. Rinse until the water runs clear.

7. Squeeze out the wet wool, and roll in a dry towel to remove excess water. Hang the wool to dry.

8. Overdye with indigo to create darker greens.

25
Hibiscus

(Hibiscus species)

- Fair lightfastness
- 4 cups of flowers
- Mordant used: For a $1/2$-yard of wool, 1 teaspoon of alum and a $1/2$-teaspoon of cream of tartar
- Maroon shades

Also called rose mallow, these red flowers produce maroon shades in the dye pot. They can be used fresh or dried. You may also pick the flowers as they fade and keep them in a pot of water with a lid on until you have enough.

The Recipe:

1. Use a $1/2$-yard of wet wool. (An alum mordant should be applied beforehand.)

2. To extract the dye from the flowers, pour boiling water over 4 cups of flowers that are contained in a mesh bag and let them steep for 30 minutes.

3. Add water to this solution to fill a large pot and heat just to a simmer for 1 hour.

4. Add the wet wool and simmer for 1 hour. Turn off the heat.

5. Let the wool cool in the pot overnight.

6. Remove the wool, and wash in water with 1 teaspoon of shampoo. Rinse until the water runs clear.

7. Squeeze out the wet wool, and roll in a dry towel to remove excess water. Hang the wool to dry.

8. Overdye with any of the reds (cochineal, lac, or madder to name a few) to create deeper red shades.

26
Hollyhock

(Alcea rosea)

- Fair lightfastness
- 4 cups of flowers
- Mordant used: For a $1/2$-yard of wool, 1 teaspoon of alum and a $1/2$-teaspoon of cream of tartar
- Mauve, maroon shades

The flowers of the hollyhock bloom on long, sturdy stalks. The blossoms grow in a variety of colors—pink, yellow, and red. The red flowers produce a maroon color and can be fresh or dried. You may also pick the flowers as they fade and keep them in a pot of water with a lid on until you have enough.

The Recipe:

1. Use a $1/2$-yard of wet wool. (An alum mordant should be applied beforehand.)

2. To extract the dye from the flowers, soak 4 cups in a mesh bag in water overnight.

3. Add water to this solution to fill a large pot and heat just to a simmer for 1 hour.

4. Add the wet wool and simmer for 1 hour. Turn off the heat.

5. Let the wool cool in the pot overnight.

6. Remove the wool, and wash in water with 1 teaspoon of shampoo. Rinse until the water runs clear.

7. Squeeze out the wet wool, and roll in a dry towel to remove excess water. Hang the wool to dry.

8. Overdye with any of the reds (cochineal, lac, or madder to name a few) to create deeper red shades.

27
Iris

(Iris, various species)

- Fair lightfastness
- 4 cups of flowers
- Mordant used: For a $1/2$-yard of wool, 1 teaspoon of alum and a $1/2$-teaspoon of cream of tartar
- Yellow shades

The root of the yellow iris is said to produce a black dye. Since iris roots are poisonous, however, I would suggest using only the flowers. Irises bloom in June and grow in moist, wet locations. You may also pick the flowers as they fade and keep them in a pot of water with a lid on until you have enough.

The Recipe:

1. Use a $1/2$-yard of wet wool. (An alum mordant should be applied beforehand.)

2. To extract the dye from the flowers, soak 4 cups in a mesh bag in water overnight.

3. Add water to this solution to fill a large pot and heat just to a simmer for 1 hour.

4. Add the wet wool and simmer for 1 hour. Turn off the heat.

5. Let the wool cool in the pot overnight.

6. Remove the wool, and wash in water with 1 teaspoon of shampoo. Rinse until the water runs clear.

7. Squeeze out the wet wool, and roll in a dry towel to remove excess water. Hang the wool to dry.

8. Overdye with indigo to create greens, and overdye with any of the reds (cochineal, lac, or madder to name a few) to create orange shades.

28
Ivy

(Hedera helix)

- Fair lightfastness
- 4 cups of leaves and vines
- Mordant used: For a $1/2$-yard of wool, 1 teaspoon of alum and a $1/2$-teaspoon of cream of tartar
- Yellow-green shades

Ivy is an evergreen vine. The leaves and vines are the source of the dye.

The Recipe:

1. Use a $1/2$-yard of wet wool. (An alum mordant should be applied beforehand.)

2. To extract the dye from the leaves and vines, soak 4 cups in a mesh bag in water overnight.

3. Add water to this solution to fill a large pot and heat just to a simmer for 1 hour.

4. Add the wet wool and simmer for 1 hour. Turn off the heat.

5. Let the wool cool in the pot overnight.

6. Remove the wool, and wash in water with 1 teaspoon of shampoo. Rinse until the water runs clear.

7. Squeeze out the wet wool, and roll in a dry towel to remove excess water. Hang the wool to dry.

8. Overdye with indigo to create darker greens.

29
Joe-Pye Weed

(Eupatorium maculatum)

- Fair lightfastness
- 4 cups of flowers
- Mordant used: For a $1/2$-yard of wool, 1 teaspoon of alum and a $1/2$-teaspoon of cream of tartar
- Yellow shades

Joe-pye weed is a tall perennial with purple flower heads. The wildflower blooms from July to September. If you can't harvest enough at one time, you may also pick the flowers as they fade and keep them in a pot of water with a lid on until you have enough.

The Recipe:

1. Use a $1/2$-yard of wet wool. (An alum mordant should be applied beforehand.)

2. To extract the dye from the flowers, soak 4 cups in a mesh bag in water overnight.

3. Add water to this solution to fill a large pot and heat just to a simmer for 1 hour.

4. Add the wet wool and simmer for 1 hour. Turn off the heat.

5. Let the wool cool in the pot overnight.

6. Remove the wool, and wash in water with 1 teaspoon of shampoo. Rinse until the water runs clear.

7. Squeeze out the wet wool, and roll in a dry towel to remove excess water. Hang the wool to dry.

8. Overdye with indigo to create greens, and overdye with any of the reds (cochineal, lac, or madder to name a few) to create orange shades.

30
Lamb's Ear

(Stacys)

- Fair lightfastness
- 4 cups of flowers and leaves
- Mordant used: For a $1/2$-yard of wool, 1 teaspoon of alum and a $1/2$-teaspoon of cream of tartar
- Yellow shades

Lamb's ear is a perennial plant with light-green leaves. The leaves are soft and velvety to the touch. Lamb's ear likes dry soil conditions, and if presented with such conditions, it will spread quickly. The flower stalks produce small blue and lavender flowers in the summer months. The leaves and flowers produce the dye.

The Recipe:

1. Use a $1/2$-yard of wet wool. (An alum mordant should be applied beforehand.)

2. To extract the dye from the flowers and leaves, soak 4 cups in a mesh bag in water overnight.

3. Add water to this solution to fill a large pot and heat just to a simmer for 1 hour.

4. Add the wet wool and simmer for 1 hour. Turn off the heat.

5. Let the wool cool in the pot overnight.

6. Remove the wool, and wash in water with 1 teaspoon of shampoo. Rinse until the water runs clear.

7. Squeeze out the wet wool, and roll in a dry towel to remove excess water. Hang the wool to dry.

8. Overdye with indigo to create greens, and overdye with any of the reds (cochineal, lac, or madder to name a few) to create orange shades.

31
Lichens

(Lasallia capulosa, Actinogyra muehlenbergii, Lobaria pulmonaria, Usnea dayspoga, Peltiger apthosa, Xanthoparmelia, Xanthoria, Parmelia omphalodes, P. Saxitilis, Roccella)

- Fair lightfastness
- 4 cups of lichens
- No mordant is necessary
- Red and purple shades

Lichens have been the source of red and purple dyes for thousands of years. Lichens are both fungal and algal organisms classified as "cryptograms." They live on rocks, trees, rotten wood, fence posts, and any other place that's convenient for them. Lichens are a food source for some animals, and some species of lichens are endangered, so care must be taken when collecting them.

Foliose lichens are the most common. They are flat and round with wavy edges and a light-green color. Crustose lichens are round and appear on trees and rocks. They are very flat and hard to remove from the surface they are living on. Fruticose lichens look like hairy shrubs and are easily collected. They produce a dye with an average lightfastness.

Lichens are easiest to collect when they are wet, but you must dry them out soon after harvesting them. They need to be crushed to release the dye.

You can extract the dye from lichens in two different ways. One is the **fermentation method**, *and the other is the* **boiling water method**. *Through the fermentation method, the colors of dye produced are pink, red, violet, and purple. The colors produced through the boiling water method are yellow, green, rust, and tan. No mordant is necessary when dyeing with lichens unless you want to alter the color.*

After you have collected the lichens, lay them out, and dry them in a warm place. If you are not going to dye with them for awhile, store them in a paper bag after they have been dried.

The old method of obtaining dye from lichens using the fermentation method was to crush them up and steep them in urine. Luckily, we now have more convenient means of fermenting lichens. The newer method of the fermentation

process is to steep the crushed lichens in a solution of ammonia and water. This vat must be stirred periodically to introduce oxygen into the water.

The Recipe:
- 4 cups of crushed lichens
- 2 cups of ammonia
- 4 cups of water

1. After the lichens have been dried, crush them up, and put them in a jar large enough to hold all the liquids needed.

2. Add the ammonia and water and stir to introduce the oxygen.

3. The mixture will smell of ammonia, so cover it up with a lid.

4. Place the jar in an area at room temperature where you will be able to stir it at least twice a day for about a week. The solution will be a dark brown color at this point.

5. After about a week the color should start to gradually change to a red color. This may take some time, so be patient.

6. Add some more ammonia if it does not start to change to a red color after about a week. It may take weeks for the full color to come out.

7. When you are ready to dye with the solution, strain the lichens out of the solution, and save them. They can be used again to make a paler dye bath. You also can dilute the dye bath with more water if the color is too strong.

8. Heat the water to a simmer, and add the wet wool.

9. Simmer for 30 minutes, and turn off the heat. (You may wish to take the wool out at this time or leave it in the dye pot to absorb more dye.)

10. Let the wool cool in the pot overnight.

11. Remove the wool, and wash it in water with 1 teaspoon of shampoo. Rinse until the water runs clear.

12. Squeeze out the wool, and roll it in a dry towel to remove the excess water. Hang to dry.

Another way to dye is without heat:

1. Add the wet wool to the ammonia, water, and lichens solution when it has reached its full red color.

2. Let the wool steep in it for several weeks.

32
Lily

(Hemerocallis fulva)

- Fair lightfastness
- 4 cups of flowers
- Mordant used: For a $1/2$-yard of wool, 1 teaspoon of alum and a $1/2$-teaspoon of cream of tartar
- Yellow shades

The daylily is a perennial flower common throughout the United States. They bloom during the summer months. True to its name, each daylily bloom only lasts one day. You may also pick the flowers as they fade and keep them in a pot of water with a lid on until you have enough.

The Recipe:

1. Use a $1/2$-yard of wet wool. (An alum mordant should be applied beforehand.)
2. To extract the dye from the flowers, soak 4 cups in a mesh bag in water overnight.
3. Add water to this solution to fill a large pot and heat just to a simmer for 1 hour.
4. Add the wet wool and simmer for 1 hour. Turn off the heat.
5. Let the wool cool in the pot overnight.
6. Remove the wool, and wash in water with 1 teaspoon of shampoo. Rinse until the water runs clear.
7. Squeeze out the wet wool, and roll in a dry towel to remove excess water. Hang the wool to dry.
8. Overdye with indigo to create greens, and overdye with any of the reds (cochineal, lac, or madder to name a few) to create orange shades.

33
Mahonia

(Mahonia species)

- Fair lightfastness
- 4 cups of berries
- Mordant used: For a $1/2$-yard of wool, 1 teaspoon of alum and a $1/2$-teaspoon of cream of tartar
- Lavender shades

Mahonias are an evergreen shrub. The berries give off a light lavender color and can be used fresh or dried. The berries are produced in the fall.

The Recipe:

1. Use a $1/2$-yard of wet wool. (An alum mordant should be applied beforehand.)
2. To extract the dye from the berries, soak 4 cups in a mesh bag in water overnight.
3. Add water to this solution to fill a large pot and heat just to a simmer for 1 hour.
4. Add the wet wool and simmer for 1 hour. Turn off the heat.
5. Let the wool cool in the pot overnight.
6. Remove the wool, and wash in water with 1 teaspoon of shampoo. Rinse until the water runs clear.
7. Squeeze out the wet wool, and roll in a dry towel to remove excess water. Hang the wool to dry.
8. Overdye with logwood to create deeper purple shades and to make the color more lightfast.

34
Marigold

(Tagetes species)

- Very good lightfastness
- 4 cups of flowers
- Mordant used: For a $1/2$-yard of wool, 1 teaspoon of alum and a $1/2$-teaspoon of cream of tartar
- Yellow shades

Marigolds originated in Central America and now are grown throughout the United States. They are annuals easily grown from seeds in abundant sunlight. Both fresh and dried flowers can be used to dye with. The yellow flowers produce the best shades of yellow.

The Recipe:

1. Use a $1/2$-yard of wet wool. (An alum mordant should be applied beforehand.)

2. To extract the dye from the flowers, soak 4 cups in a mesh bag in water overnight.

3. Add water to this solution to fill a large pot and heat just to a simmer for 1 hour.

4. Add the wet wool and simmer for 1 hour. Turn off the heat.

5. Let the wool cool in the pot overnight.

6. Remove the wool, and wash in water with 1 teaspoon of shampoo. Rinse until the water runs clear.

7. Squeeze out the wet wool, and roll in a dry towel to remove excess water. Hang the wool to dry.

8. Overdye with indigo to create greens, and overdye with any of the reds (cochineal, lac, or madder to name a few) to create orange shades.

35
Mint

(Mentha piperita, Mentha spicata)

- Fair lightfastness
- 4 cups of mint
- Mordant used: For a $1/2$-yard of wool, 1 teaspoon of alum and a $1/2$-teaspoon of cream of tartar
- Yellow shades

This perennial herb is typically known for its pleasant smell and taste, but the leaves can make an equally pleasant yellow dye. Since mint is a ground cover that can blanket a whole area rapidly, you should have no problem finding an abundance of mint if you look in the right places.

The Recipe:

1. Use a $1/2$-yard of wet wool. (An alum mordant should be applied beforehand.)

2. To extract the dye from the herb, soak 4 cups in a mesh bag in water overnight.

3. Add water to this solution to fill a large pot and heat just to a simmer for 1 hour.

4. Add the wet wool and simmer for 1 hour. Turn off the heat.

5. Let the wool cool in the pot overnight.

6. Remove the wool, and wash in water with 1 teaspoon of shampoo. Rinse until the water runs clear.

7. Squeeze out the wet wool, and roll in a dry towel to remove excess water. Hang the wool to dry.

8. Overdye with indigo to create greens, and overdye with any of the reds (cochineal, lac, or madder to name a few) to create orange shades.

36
Mullein

(Verbascum thapsus)

- Very good lightfastness
- 4 cups of flowers and leaves
- Mordant used: For a $1/2$-yard of wool, 1 teaspoon of alum and a $1/2$-teaspoon of cream of tartar
- Purple shades

Mulleins typically grow in the wild, but you can also grow this biennial in your garden if you so desire. They can grow up to 8 feet tall. Interestingly enough, mullein reseeds itself, and the leaves have the soft feel of an old flannel shirt. Mulleins bloom in July through August. The leaves and stalks are used in the dyeing process.

The Recipe:

1. Use a $1/2$-yard of wet wool. (An alum mordant should be applied beforehand.)

2. To extract the dye from the stalks and leaves, chop them up, and soak 4 cups in a mesh bag in water overnight.

3. Add water to this solution to fill a large pot and heat just to a simmer for 1 hour.

4. Add the wet wool and simmer for 1 hour. Turn off the heat.

5. Let the wool cool in the pot overnight.

6. Remove the wool, and wash in water with 1 teaspoon of shampoo. Rinse until the water runs clear.

7. Squeeze out the wet wool, and roll in a dry towel to remove excess water. Hang the wool to dry.

8. Overdye with logwood to create deeper purple shades and to make the color more lightfast.

37
Mushrooms

(various varieties)

- Fair lightfastness
- 4 cups of chopped mushrooms
- Mordant used: For a $1/2$-yard of wool, 1 teaspoon of alum and a $1/2$-teaspoon of cream of tartar
- Tan, pink, purple, yellow, green, and grey shades

Certain types of mushrooms can be used in dyeing, but because of the safety issues involved with picking mushrooms in the wild, I would highly recommend sticking with the safe, nontoxic mushrooms you can find in the produce section of your grocery store. These are a much safer bet than picking potentially poisonous mushrooms in the wild. Sometimes, even if you're 99 percent certain the wild mushroom is safe, you cannot be positive.

The Recipe:

1. Chop up 4 cups of mushrooms, and soak them in a mesh bag in water with a lid on for at least two days.

2. Simmer them in a large pot of water for 1 hour. Then add your wet wool.

3. Simmer for another 30 minutes, and turn off the heat.

4. Allow the wool to cool overnight in the pot.

5. Remove the wool, and wash with 1 teaspoon of shampoo. Rinse until the water runs clear.

6. Squeeze out the wet wool, and roll it in a dry towel to remove excess water. Hang the wool to dry.

7. *Agaricus campestris*, the common mushrooms you find in the grocery store, produce shades of yellow with an alum mordant. They produce gold, rust, and brown with the other mordants.

38
Nasturtium

(Nasturtium officinale)

- Fair lightfastness
- 4 cups of flowers
- Mordant used: For a $1/2$-yard of wool, 1 teaspoon of alum and a $1/2$-teaspoon of cream of tartar
- Yellow shades

Nasturtiums are annual garden flowers. The plant itself grows to about 18 inches high, and the flowers come in shades of white, pink, red, orange, yellow, and violet. The dye is in the flowers. If you cannot harvest enough nasturtiums at one time, you may also pick the flowers as they fade and keep them in a pot of water with a lid on until you have enough.

The Recipe:

1. Use a $1/2$-yard of wet wool. (An alum mordant should be applied beforehand.)

2. To extract the dye from the flowers, soak 4 cups in a mesh bag in water overnight.

3. Add water to this solution to fill a large pot and heat just to a simmer for 1 hour.

4. Add the wet wool and simmer for 1 hour. Turn off the heat.

5. Let the wool cool in the pot overnight.

6. Remove the wool, and wash in water with 1 teaspoon of shampoo. Rinse until the water runs clear.

7. Squeeze out the wet wool, and roll in a dry towel to remove excess water. Hang the wool to dry.

8. Overdye with indigo to create greens, and overdye with any of the reds (cochineal, lac, or madder to name a few) to create orange shades.

39
Nettle

(Urtica dioica)

- Fair lightfastness
- 4 cups of leaves and stalks
- Mordant used: For a $1/2$-yard of wool, 1 teaspoon of alum and a $1/2$-teaspoon of cream of tartar
- Yellow shades

The stinging nettle is considered a weed, but the leaves and stalks can make a nice yellow dye. Since it has tiny thorns along the leaves, be sure to wear gloves when picking it.

The Recipe:

1. Use a $1/2$-yard of wet wool. (An alum mordant should be applied beforehand.)

2. To extract the dye from the leaves and stalks, soak 4 cups in a mesh bag in water overnight.

3. Add water to this solution to fill a large pot and heat just to a simmer for 1 hour.

4. Add the wet wool and simmer for 1 hour. Turn off the heat.

5. Let the wool cool in the pot overnight.

6. Remove the wool, and wash in water with 1 teaspoon of shampoo. Rinse until the water runs clear.

7. Squeeze out the wet wool, and roll in a dry towel to remove excess water. Hang the wool to dry.

8. Overdye with indigo to create greens, and overdye with any of the reds (cochineal, lac, or madder to name a few) to create orange shades.

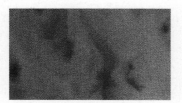

40
Red Onion Skins

(Allium cepa)

- Very good lightfastness
- 2 cups of dried skins
- No mordant is necessary
- Green, purple, and rust shades

I obtain my onion skins from the grocery store. Sometimes, I simply pick up the skins that have fallen off the onions. I also ask the produce manager to save the box that the onions have been packed in because most of the onion skins often are left in the box to be thrown away. To legitimize myself, I always buy one whole onion and fill the rest of the bag with skins. I always get funny looks from the checkout person in the grocery store when I do this, but it's worth it when I get home to the dye pot.

When I dye with red onion skins, I'm never quite sure what color I'm going to get. In the past, they have produced rust, green, and purple shades. Red onion skins aren't consistent, but at least they keep things interesting! You will notice one consistent thing when you're dyeing with onion skins, however. The pleasant aroma smells like you're making a pot of French Onion soup.

The Recipe:

1. Simmer the skins in a mesh bag for 15 minutes in a large pot of water with the lid on.

2. Add the wet wool, and simmer for 30 minutes.

3. Turn off heat, and leave the wool in the pot overnight to cool.

4. Wash the dyed wool in water with 1 teaspoon of shampoo, and rinse until the water runs clear.

5. Squeeze out the wet wool, and roll it in a dry towel to remove the excess water. Hang the wool to dry.

6. The casserole method of dyeing works really well with onion skins. (*For more information on the casserole method, see page 11*)

41
Yellow Onion Skins

(Allium cepa)

- Very good lightfastness
- 2 cups of dried skins
- No mordant is necessary
- Yellow and orange shades

Follow the same process as with red onion skins. Overdye the yellow wool with indigo to create a green color, or overdye with any of the reds (like madder, lac or brazilwood) to create orange shades.

42
Pansy

(viola, various species)

- Fair lightfastness
- 4 cups of flowers
- Mordant used: For a $1/2$-yard of wool, 1 teaspoon of alum and a $1/2$-teaspoon of cream of tartar
- Yellow, beige, and pink shades

This common garden flower blooms in the spring and comes in a variety of colors. If you can't pick enough at one time for dyeing, you may also pick the flowers as they fade and keep them in a pot of water with a lid on until you have enough.

The Recipe:

1. Use a $1/2$-yard of wet wool. (An alum mordant should be applied beforehand.)

2. To extract the dye from the flowers, soak 4 cups in a mesh bag in water overnight.

3. Add water to this solution to fill a large pot and heat just to a simmer for 1 hour.

4. Add the wet wool and simmer for 1 hour. Turn off the heat.

5. Let the wool cool in the pot overnight.

6. Remove the wool, and wash in water with 1 teaspoon of shampoo. Rinse until the water runs clear.

7. Squeeze out the wet wool, and roll in a dry towel to remove excess water. Hang the wool to dry.

43
Peony

(Paeonia lactiflora)

- Fair lightfastness
- 4 cups of flowers
- Mordant used: For a $1/2$-yard of wool, 1 teaspoon of alum and a $1/2$-teaspoon of cream of tartar
- Yellow shades

Peonies are perennials with large flowers. They blossom in the spring in shades of white, pink, and red. The dye is in the flowers.

If you can't find enough peonies for dyeing all at once, you may also pick the flowers as they fade and keep them in a pot of water with a lid on until you have enough.

The Recipe:

1. Use a $1/2$-yard of wet wool. (An alum mordant should be applied beforehand.)

2. To extract the dye from the flowers, soak 4 cups in a mesh bag in water overnight.

3. Add water to this solution to fill a large pot and heat just to a simmer for 1 hour.

4. Add the wet wool and simmer for 1 hour. Turn off the heat.

5. Let the wool cool in the pot overnight.

6. Remove the wool, and wash in water with 1 teaspoon of shampoo. Rinse until the water runs clear.

7. Squeeze out the wet wool, and roll in a dry towel to remove excess water. Hang the wool to dry.

8. Overdye with indigo to create greens, and overdye with any of the reds (cochineal, lac, or madder to name a few) to create orange shades.

44
Petunia

(Petunia)

- Fair lightfastness
- 4 cups of flowers
- Mordant used: For a $^1/_2$-yard of wool, 1 teaspoon of alum and a $^1/_2$-teaspoon of cream of tartar
- Yellow shades

Petunias are annual flowers that come in a plethora of different shades and colors. The flowers are what produce the dye, but the dye is not very lightfast and will fade over time. If you can't pick enough petunias at one time, you may also pick the flowers as they fade and keep them in a pot of water with a lid on until you have enough.

The Recipe:

1. Use a $^1/_2$-yard of wet wool. (An alum mordant should be applied beforehand.)

2. To extract the dye from the flowers, soak 4 cups in a mesh bag in water overnight.

3. Add water to this solution to fill a large pot and heat just to a simmer for 1 hour.

4. Add the wet wool and simmer for 1 hour. Turn off the heat.

5. Let the wool cool in the pot overnight.

6. Remove the wool, and wash in water with 1 teaspoon of shampoo. Rinse until the water runs clear.

7. Squeeze out the wet wool, and roll in a dry towel to remove excess water. Hang the wool to dry.

8. Overdye with indigo to create greens, and overdye with any of the reds (cochineal, lac, or madder to name a few) to create orange shades.

45
Plantain

(Plantage major)

- Fair lightfastness
- 4 cups of leaves
- Mordant used: For a $^1/_2$-yard of wool, 1 teaspoon of alum and a $^1/_2$-teaspoon of cream of tartar
- Yellow-green shades

Plantain is a common weed with ribbed leaves that grow flat to the ground. Like most weeds, plantains offer you a variety of picking seasons. It grows in the spring, summer, and fall. The young leaves often are used as a food source.

The Recipe:

1. Use a $^1/_2$-yard of wet wool. (An alum mordant should be applied beforehand.)

2. To extract the dye from the leaves, soak 4 cups in a mesh bag in water overnight.

3. Add water to this solution to fill a large pot and heat just to a simmer for 1 hour.

4. Add the wet wool and simmer for 1 hour. Turn off the heat.

5. Let the wool cool in the pot overnight.

6. Remove the wool, and wash in water with 1 teaspoon of shampoo. Rinse until the water runs clear.

7. Squeeze out the wet wool, and roll in a dry towel to remove excess water. Hang the wool to dry.

8. Overdye with indigo to create darker greens.

46
Pokeberry

(Phytolacca americana)

- Fair lightfastness
- 4 cups of berries
- Mordant used: For a $1/2$-yard of wool, 1 teaspoon of alum and a $1/2$-teaspoon of cream of tartar
- Red shades

Also called pokeweed, pokeberry is a perennial shrub that produces purple berries that the birds love. Don't take a hint from the birds, however. The berries are poisonous if ingested by humans. Pokeberry is a dye our ancestors used, but there is some controversy over whether the dye is fast or fugitive (fades).

The Recipe:

1. Use a $1/2$-yard of wet wool. (An alum mordant should be applied beforehand.)

2. To extract the dye from the berries, soak 4 cups in a mesh bag in water overnight.

3. Add water to this solution to fill a large pot and heat just to a simmer for 1 hour.

4. Add the wet wool and simmer for 1 hour. Turn off the heat.

5. Let the wool cool in the pot overnight.

6. Remove the wool, and wash in water with 1 teaspoon of shampoo. Rinse until the water runs clear.

7. Squeeze out the wet wool, and roll in a dry towel to remove excess water. Hang the wool to dry.

8. You could overdye with lac or madder to make it more lightfast.

47
Pomegranate

(Punica granatum)

- Fair lightfastness
- 4 cups of chopped fruit
- Mordant used: For a $1/2$-yard of wool, 1 teaspoon of alum and a $1/2$-teaspoon of cream of tartar
- Yellow and tan shades

Pomegranate dye comes from the edible fruit, which ripens in early fall on a small tree found in Europe, the Middle East, India, Asia, the West Indies, and North Africa. Of course, if you don't have the means to travel around the world to gather your pomegranates, you should be able to find them in abundance at a local grocery store. Pomegranates can be used fresh or dried, and they can also be bought in powdered form.

The Recipe:

1. Use a $1/2$-yard of wet wool. (An alum mordant should be applied beforehand.)

2. To extract the dye from the fruit, chop it up, and soak 4 cups in a mesh bag in water overnight.

3. Add water to this solution to fill a large pot and heat just to a simmer for 1 hour.

4. Add the wet wool and simmer for 1 hour. Turn off the heat.

5. Let the wool cool in the pot overnight.

6. Remove the wool, and wash in water with 1 teaspoon of shampoo. Rinse until the water runs clear.

7. Squeeze out the wet wool, and roll in a dry towel to remove excess water. Hang the wool to dry.

8. A greenish-brown color will be produced if you use an iron mordant. Overdye with indigo to make green shades.

48
Poppy

(Papaver orientale)

- Fair lightfastness
- 4 cups of flowers
- Mordant used: For a $1/2$-yard of wool, 1 teaspoon of alum and a $1/2$-teaspoon of cream of tartar
- Beige shades

Poppies are perennials with flowers in shades of white, pink, salmon, orange, and red. They bloom in June, and the flowers are the dye source. If you can't pick enough poppies at one time for dyeing, you may also pick the flowers as they fade and keep them in a pot of water with a lid on until you have enough.

The Recipe:

1. Use a $1/2$-yard of wet wool. (An alum mordant should be applied beforehand.)

2. To extract the dye from the flowers, soak 4 cups in a mesh bag in water overnight.

3. Add water to this solution to fill a large pot and heat just to a simmer for 1 hour.

4. Add the wet wool and simmer for 1 hour. Turn off the heat.

5. Let the wool cool in the pot overnight.

6. Remove the wool, and wash in water with 1 teaspoon of shampoo. Rinse until the water runs clear.

7. Squeeze out the wet wool, and roll in a dry towel to remove excess water. Hang the wool to dry.

49
Primrose

(Primula)

- Fair lightfastness
- 4 cups of flowers
- Mordant used: For a $1/2$-yard of wool, 1 teaspoon of alum and a $1/2$-teaspoon of cream of tartar
- Pale yellow shades

Primrose flowers bloom on a spike in a multitude of different colors. They are perennials and bloom in May and June. The flowers are used in the dyeing process. You may also pick the flowers as they fade and keep them in a pot of water with a lid on until you have enough.

The Recipe:

1. Use a $1/2$-yard of wet wool. (An alum mordant should be applied beforehand.)

2. To extract the dye from the flowers, soak 4 cups in a mesh bag in water overnight.

3. Add water to this solution to fill a large pot and heat just to a simmer for 1 hour.

4. Add the wet wool and simmer for 1 hour. Turn off the heat.

5. Let the wool cool in the pot overnight.

6. Remove the wool, and wash in water with 1 teaspoon of shampoo. Rinse until the water runs clear.

7. Squeeze out the wet wool, and roll in a dry towel to remove excess water. Hang the wool to dry.

8. Overdye with indigo to create greens, and overdye with any of the reds (cochineal, lac, or madder to name a few) to create orange shades.

50
Purslane

(Portacula oleracea)

- Fair lightfastness
- 4 cups of leaves
- Mordant used: For a $1/2$-yard of wool,
  1 teaspoon of alum and a $1/2$-teaspoon of cream
  of tartar
- Yellow shades

Purslane once was considered a weed, but it 's now a popular wild food that you might find in salad mixes. Purslane grows low to the ground, and the stems are often thick and rubbery. Purslane's dye is in the leaves.

The Recipe:

1. Use a $1/2$-yard of wet wool. (An alum mordant should be applied beforehand.)

2. To extract the dye from the leaves, soak 4 cups in a mesh bag in water overnight.

3. Add water to this solution to fill a large pot and heat just to a simmer for 1 hour.

4. Add the wet wool and simmer for 1 hour. Turn off the heat.

5. Let the wool cool in the pot overnight.

6. Remove the wool, and wash in water with 1 teaspoon of shampoo. Rinse until the water runs clear.

7. Squeeze out the wet wool, and roll in a dry towel to remove excess water. Hang the wool to dry.

8. Overdye with indigo to create greens, and overdye with any of the reds (cochineal, lac, or madder to name a few) to create orange shades.

51
Queen Anne's Lace

(Daucus carota)

- Fair lightfastness
- 4 cups of flowers
- Mordant used: For a $1/2$-yard of wool,
  1 teaspoon of alum and a $1/2$-teaspoon of cream
  of tartar
- Yellow-green shades

Also called wild carrot, Queen Anne's lace offers up colors similar to store-bought carrot tops when thrown in the dye pot. The flowers are the source of the dye and are best used fresh. You may also pick the flowers as they fade and keep them in a pot of water with a lid on until you have enough.

The Recipe:

1. Use a $1/2$-yard of wet wool. (An alum mordant should be applied beforehand.)

2. To extract the dye from the flowers, soak 4 cups in a mesh bag in water overnight.

3. Add water to this solution to fill a large pot and heat just to a simmer for 1 hour.

4. Add the wet wool and simmer for 1 hour. Turn off the heat.

5. Let the wool cool in the pot overnight.

6. Remove the wool, and wash in water with 1 teaspoon of shampoo. Rinse until the water runs clear.

7. Squeeze out the wet wool, and roll in a dry towel to remove excess water. Hang the wool to dry.

8. Overdye with indigo to create darker greens.

52
Rhododendron

(Rhododendron)

- Fair lightfastness
- 4 cups of chopped leaves
- Mordant used: For a $1/2$-yard of wool, 1 teaspoon of alum and a $1/2$-teaspoon of cream of tartar
- Yellow shades

This evergreen shrub produces beautiful blossoms, but do not let your dyer's eyes be fooled. It is the leaves that are the dye source of this plant, not the flowers.

The Recipe:

1. Use a $1/2$-yard of wet wool. (An alum mordant should be applied beforehand.)

2. The leaves are a little tough, so chop them up and soak in water in a mesh bag for a couple of days.

3. Add water to this solution to fill a large pot and heat just to a simmer for 1 hour.

4. Add the wet wool and simmer for 1 hour. Turn off the heat.

5. Let the wool cool in the pot overnight.

6. Remove the wool, and wash in water with 1 teaspoon of shampoo. Rinse until the water runs clear.

7. Squeeze out the wet wool, and roll in a dry towel to remove excess water. Hang the wool to dry.

8. Overdye with indigo to create greens, and overdye with any of the reds (cochineal, lac, or madder to name a few) to create orange shades.

53
Rhubarb

(Rheum species)

- Fair lightfastness
- 4 cups of leaves or roots
- No mordant is necessary
- Yellow-green and orange shades

Rhubarb stems can be made into jellies and pies, but the leaves and roots are the source of a nice yellow or orange dye. If you're eating rhubarb, however, stick to the stem. The leaves are poisonous if ingested. Yellow-green shades are achieved when using the leaves and orange shades when using the roots. Use rubber gloves when handling the leaves.

The Recipe:

1. Use a $1/2$-yard of wet wool. (No mordant is necessary with rhubarb.)

2. To extract the dye from the leaves or roots, soak 4 cups in a mesh bag in water overnight.

3. Add water to this solution to fill a large pot and heat just to a simmer for 1 hour.

4. Add the wet wool and simmer for 1 hour. Turn off the heat.

5. Let the wool cool in the pot overnight.

6. Remove the wool, and wash in water with 1 teaspoon of shampoo. Rinse until the water runs clear.

7. Squeeze out the wet wool, and roll in a dry towel to remove excess water. Hang the wool to dry.

8. Overdye with indigo to create greens, and overdye with any of the reds (cochineal, lac, or madder to name a few) to create deeper orange shades.

54
Rose

(Rosa)

- Fair lightfastness
- 4 cups of flowers
- Mordant used: For a $^1/_2$-yard of wool,
  1 teaspoon of alum and a $^1/_2$-teaspoon of cream
  of tartar
- Yellow shades

It's no surprise that the dye from this flowering shrub is in the beautiful petals (where else?). But if you can't bear to pick all your beautiful rose petals all at once, you may also pick the flowers as they fade and keep them in a pot of water with a lid on until you have enough.

The Recipe:

1. Use a $^1/_2$-yard of wet wool. (An alum mordant should be applied beforehand.)

2. To extract the dye from the flowers, soak 4 cups in a mesh bag in water overnight.

3. Add water to this solution to fill a large pot and heat just to a simmer for 1 hour.

4. Add the wet wool and simmer for 1 hour. Turn off the heat.

5. Let the wool cool in the pot overnight.

6. Remove the wool, and wash in water with 1 teaspoon of shampoo. Rinse until the water runs clear.

7. Squeeze out the wet wool, and roll in a dry towel to remove excess water. Hang the wool to dry.

8. Overdye with indigo to create greens, and overdye with any of the reds (cochineal, lac, or madder to name a few) to create orange shades.

55
Safflower

(Carthamus tinctorius)

- Fair lightfastness
- 4 cups of flowers
- Mordant used: For a $^1/_2$-yard of wool,
  1 teaspoon of alum and a $^1/_2$-teaspoon of cream
  of tartar
- Yellow shades

Most people don't know this minor bit of historical trivia, but safflower is actually where the term "red tape" originates. Safflower historically was cultivated in India, China, Egypt, and Europe, and in these countries, ribbons to bind legal documents were dyed pink with safflower.

The safflower plant is actually a hardy annual thistle that can grow 2 to 3 feet tall. You can use fresh or dried flowers for the dye. You may also pick the flowers as they fade and keep them in a pot of water with a lid on until you have enough.

The Recipe:

1. Use a $^1/_2$-yard of wet wool. (An alum mordant should be applied beforehand.)

2. To extract the dye from the flowers, soak 4 cups in a mesh bag in water overnight.

3. Add water to this solution to fill a large pot and heat just to a simmer for 1 hour.

4. Add the wet wool and simmer for 1 hour. Turn off the heat.

5. Let the wool cool in the pot overnight.

6. Remove the wool, and wash in water with 1 teaspoon of shampoo. Rinse until the water runs clear.

7. Squeeze out the wet wool, and roll in a dry towel to remove excess water. Hang the wool to dry.

8. Overdye with indigo to create greens, and overdye with any of the reds (cochineal, lac, or madder to name a few) to create orange shades.

56
Sage

(Salvia officinalis)

- Fair lightfastness
- 4 cups of leaves
- Mordant used: For a $1/2$-yard of wool, 1 teaspoon of alum and a $1/2$-teaspoon of cream of tartar
- Yellow-green shades

This common herb can be grown fresh in your garden or found in the grocery store. Both the fresh leaves and the powdered form of the herb will work well in your dye pot.

The Recipe:

1. Use a $1/2$-yard of wet wool. (An alum mordant should be applied beforehand.)

2. To extract the dye from the leaves, soak 4 cups in a mesh bag in water overnight.

3. Add water to this solution to fill a large pot and heat just to a simmer for 1 hour.

4. Add the wet wool and simmer for 1 hour. Turn off the heat.

5. Let the wool cool in the pot overnight.

6. Remove the wool, and wash in water with 1 teaspoon of shampoo. Rinse until the water runs clear.

7. Squeeze out the wet wool, and roll in a dry towel to remove excess water. Hang the wool to dry.

8. Overdye with indigo to create darker greens.

57
Saint-John's-Wort

(Hypericum perforatum)

- Fair lightfastness
- 4 cups of flowers
- Mordant used: For a $1/2$-yard of wool, 1 teaspoon of alum and a $1/2$-teaspoon of cream of tartar
- Yellow shades

Saint-John's-wort is a perennial plant with yellow flowers that bloom all summer long. Use these flowers for the dye. You may also pick the flowers as they fade and keep them in a pot of water with a lid on until you have enough.

The Recipe:

1. Use a $1/2$-yard of wet wool. (An alum mordant should be applied beforehand.)

2. To extract the dye from the flowers, soak 4 cups in a mesh bag in water overnight.

3. Add water to this solution to fill a large pot and heat just to a simmer for 1 hour.

4. Add the wet wool and simmer for 1 hour. Turn off the heat.

5. Let the wool cool in the pot overnight.

6. Remove the wool, and wash in water with 1 teaspoon of shampoo. Rinse until the water runs clear.

7. Squeeze out the wet wool, and roll in a dry towel to remove excess water. Hang the wool to dry.

8. Overdye with indigo to create greens, and overdye with any of the reds (cochineal, lac, or madder to name a few) to create orange shades.

58
Shasta Daisy

(Chrysanthemum, various species)

- Fair lightfastness
- 4 cups of flowers
- Mordant used: For a $1/2$-yard of wool, 1 teaspoon of alum and a $1/2$-teaspoon of cream of tartar
- Pale yellow shades

The shasta daisy is a perennial plant with white, pink, yellow, and blue flowers. Use the flowers for the dye. You may also pick the flowers as they fade and keep them in a pot of water with a lid on until you have enough.

The Recipe:

1. Use a $1/2$-yard of wet wool. (An alum mordant should be applied beforehand.)

2. To extract the dye from the flowers, soak 4 cups in a mesh bag in water overnight.

3. Add water to this solution to fill a large pot and heat just to a simmer for 1 hour.

4. Add the wet wool and simmer for 1 hour. Turn off the heat.

5. Let the wool cool in the pot overnight.

6. Remove the wool, and wash in water with 1 teaspoon of shampoo. Rinse until the water runs clear.

7. Squeeze out the wet wool, and roll in a dry towel to remove excess water. Hang the wool to dry.

8. Overdye with indigo to create greens, and overdye with any of the reds (cochineal, lac, or madder to name a few) to create orange shades.

59
Sorrel

(Rumex acetosella)

- Fair lightfastness
- 4 cups of leaves
- Mordant used: For a $1/2$-yard of wool, 1 teaspoon of alum and a $1/2$-teaspoon of cream of tartar
- Yellow-green shades

Sorrel is a perennial plant that is often used as a food source in a salad. You'll know a sorrel leaf because it's in the shape of an arrowhead. These fresh leaves are the source of your sorrel dye.

The Recipe:

1. Use a $1/2$-yard of wet wool. (An alum mordant should be applied beforehand.)

2. To extract the dye from the leaves, soak 4 cups in a mesh bag in water overnight.

3. Add water to this solution to fill a large pot and heat just to a simmer for 1 hour.

4. Add the wet wool and simmer for 1 hour. Turn off the heat.

5. Let the wool cool in the pot overnight.

6. Remove the wool, and wash in water with 1 teaspoon of shampoo. Rinse until the water runs clear.

7. Squeeze out the wet wool, and roll in a dry towel to remove excess water. Hang the wool to dry.

8. Overdye with indigo to create darker greens.

60
Squash

(Cucurbita)

- Fair lightfastness
- 4 cups of peels
- Mordant used: For a $1/2$-yard of wool, 1 teaspoon of alum and a $1/2$-teaspoon of cream of tartar
- Yellow shades

Our round friend, the squash, and his counterpart, the pumpkin, can both be used for this dye recipe. Either one should be easy to grow in your garden or find at the grocery store at the right time of the year. The skins of the squash or pumpkins are used as the dye source.

The Recipe:

1. Use a $1/2$-yard of wet wool. (An alum mordant should be applied beforehand.)

2. To extract the dye from the peels, soak 4 cups in a mesh bag in water overnight.

3. Add water to this solution to fill a large pot and heat just to a simmer for 1 hour.

4. Add the wet wool and simmer for 1 hour. Turn off the heat.

5. Let the wool cool in the pot overnight.

6. Remove the wool, and wash in water with 1 teaspoon of shampoo. Rinse until the water runs clear.

7. Squeeze out the wet wool, and roll in a dry towel to remove excess water. Hang the wool to dry.

8. Overdye with indigo to create greens, and overdye with any of the reds (cochineal, lac, or madder to name a few) to create orange shades.

61
Sumac

(Rhus glabra)

- Very good lightfastness
- 4 cups of berries
- Mordant used: For a $1/2$-yard of wool, 1 teaspoon of alum and a $1/2$-teaspoon of cream of tartar
- Tan, brown shades

One of the largest of our dye sources, sumac is a perennial shrub that actually can grow up to 20 feet tall. Sumac is geographically diverse, and it grows in the United States, Canada, Europe, Asia, and Africa. An American Indian tribe, the Ojibas, used the berries as a drink, and the Kiowa Indians used the sumac leaves along with tobacco in their pipes. Sumac is also a mordant in itself, but the tan and brown dye you can extract from the berries is what we'll touch on here.

The Recipe:

1. Use a $1/2$-yard of wet wool. (An alum mordant should be applied beforehand.)

2. To extract the dye from the berries, crush and soak 4 cups in a mesh bag in water overnight.

3. Add water to this solution to fill a large pot and heat just to a simmer for 1 hour.

4. Add the wet wool and simmer for 1 hour. Turn off the heat.

5. Let the wool cool in the pot overnight.

6. Remove the wool, and wash in water with 1 teaspoon of shampoo. Rinse until the water runs clear.

7. Squeeze out the wet wool, and roll in a dry towel to remove excess water. Hang the wool to dry.

8. I achieved bronze shades when I added 2 teaspoons of a copper mordant at the end of the dyeing process.

62
Sunflower

(Helianthus annuus)

- Fair lightfastness
- 4 cups of flowers and stalks
- Mordant used: For a $^1/_2$-yard of wool, 1 teaspoon of alum and a $^1/_2$-teaspoon of cream of tartar
- Yellow shades

These tall-growing annuals produce flowers in the red, orange, and yellow range. The seeds are frequently used as a food source, but the dye we're after is in the flowers and stalks. If you can't pick enough sunflowers at one time, you may also pick the flowers as they fade and keep them in a pot of water with a lid on until you have enough.

The Recipe:

1. Use a $^1/_2$-yard of wet wool. (An alum mordant should be applied beforehand.)

2. To extract the dye from the flowers and stalks, soak 4 cups in a mesh bag in water overnight.

3. Add water to this solution to fill a large pot and heat just to a simmer for 1 hour.

4. Add the wet wool and simmer for 1 hour. Turn off the heat.

5. Let the wool cool in the pot overnight.

6. Remove the wool, and wash in water with 1 teaspoon of shampoo. Rinse until the water runs clear.

7. Squeeze out the wet wool, and roll in a dry towel to remove excess water. Hang the wool to dry.

8. Overdye with indigo to create greens, and overdye with any of the reds (cochineal, lac, or madder to name a few) to create orange shades. A final rinse with baking soda after dyeing will change the color to yellow-green.

63
Tansy

(Tanacetum vulgare)

- Fair lightfastness
- 4 cups of flowers and leaves
- Mordant used: For a $^1/_2$-yard of wool, 1 teaspoon of alum and a $^1/_2$-teaspoon of cream of tartar
- Yellow-green shades

Tansy is an annual herb used as a food source. The dye comes from the flowers and leaves.

The Recipe:

1. Use a $^1/_2$-yard of wet wool. (An alum mordant should be applied beforehand.)

2. To extract the dye from the flowers and leaves, soak 4 cups in a mesh bag in water overnight.

3. Add water to this solution to fill a large pot and heat just to a simmer for 1 hour.

4. Add the wet wool and simmer for 1 hour. Turn off the heat.

5. Let the wool cool in the pot overnight.

6. Remove the wool, and wash in water with 1 teaspoon of shampoo. Rinse until the water runs clear.

7. Squeeze out the wet wool, and roll in a dry towel to remove excess water. Hang the wool to dry.

8. Overdye with indigo to create darker greens.

64
Tea

(Thea sinensis)

- Very good lightfastness
- 5 to 10 fresh or used tea bags
- No mordant is necessary
- Tan shades

Rather than travel the world is search of fresh tea leaves, simply use five or more fresh or used tea bags when dyeing with tea. Tea also works effectively for the casserole dyeing method. (See page 11.) To do this, tear open the bags and sprinkle the tea leaves between the layers of wool.

The Recipe:

1. Use a $1/2$-yard of wet wool. (No mordant is necessary.)

2. To extract the dye from the leaves, pour boiling water over the 5 to 10 tea bags, and let it steep for 15 minutes.

3. Add water to this solution to fill a large pot, and simmer for 1 hour.

4. Add the wet wool, and simmer for 1 hour. Turn off the heat.

5. Let the wool cool in the pot overnight.

6. Remove the wool, and wash in water with 1 teaspoon of shampoo. Rinse until the water runs clear.

7. Squeeze out the wet wool and roll in a dry towel to remove excess water. Hang the wool to dry.

8. Add an alum and iron mordant to achieve a greenish-brown color.

(Note: Fresh or used coffee grinds can also be used in the same method as tea. Just put the grounds in a mesh bag. Tan and brown shades will also occur with coffee.)

65
Tomato

(Solanum lycopersicum)

- Fair lightfastness
- $1/2$ a large pot of vines and leaves
- Mordant used: For a $1/2$-yard of wool, 1 teaspoon of alum and a $1/2$-teaspoon of cream of tartar
- Yellow-green shades

The tomato vine, rather than the fruit, is the source of the tomato dye. As a result, you might need to find your tomatoes fresh, or buy the tomatoes at market that are still clustered on the vine.

The Recipe:

1. Use a $1/2$-yard of wet wool. (An alum mordant should be applied beforehand.)

2. To extract the dye from the vines and leaves, chop up enough to fill half of a large pot, and soak them in a mesh bag in water overnight.

3. Add water to this solution to fill a large pot and heat just to a simmer for 1 hour.

4. Add the wet wool and simmer for 1 hour. Turn off the heat.

5. Let the wool cool in the pot overnight.

6. Remove the wool, and wash in water with 1 teaspoon of shampoo. Rinse until the water runs clear.

7. Squeeze out the wet wool, and roll in a dry towel to remove excess water. Hang the wool to dry.

8. Overdye with indigo to create darker greens.

66
Tulip

(Tulipa)

- Fair lightfastness
- 4 cups of flowers
- Mordant used: For a $1/2$-yard of wool, 1 teaspoon of alum and a $1/2$-teaspoon of cream of tartar
- Yellow shades

The tulip is a flowering bulb with a variety of flower colors. The tulip flowers are the source of the dye, and you may pick the flowers as they fade and keep them in a pot of water with a lid on until you have enough. You can also combine daffodil and tulip flowers to make a nice yellow dye.

The Recipe:

1. Use a $1/2$-yard of wet wool. (An alum mordant should be applied beforehand.)

2. To extract the dye from the flowers, soak 4 cups in a mesh bag in water overnight.

3. Add water to this solution to fill a large pot and heat just to a simmer for 1 hour.

4. Add the wet wool and simmer for 1 hour. Turn off the heat.

5. Let the wool cool in the pot overnight.

6. Remove the wool, and wash in water with 1 teaspoon of shampoo. Rinse until the water runs clear.

7. Squeeze out the wet wool, and roll in a dry towel to remove excess water. Hang the wool to dry.

8. Overdye with indigo to create greens, and overdye with any of the reds (cochineal, lac, or madder to name a few) to create orange shades.

67
Turmeric

(Curcuma longa)

- Very good lightfastness
- 1 tablespoon of powdered turmeric
- Mordant used: For a $1/2$-yard of wool, 1 teaspoon of alum and a $1/2$-teaspoon of cream of tartar
- Bright lemon yellow shades

Turmeric is a spice in the ginger family. The plant grows natively in Asia, but it can be purchased in any grocery store. The tuber of the plant is used as the dye.

The Recipe:

1. Use a $1/2$-yard of wet wool. (An alum mordant should be applied beforehand.)

2. Add 1 tablespoon of powdered turmeric to a large pot of water, and simmer for 15 minutes.

3. Add the wet wool and simmer for 30 minutes. Turn off the heat.

4. Let the wool cool in the pot overnight.

5. Remove the wool, and wash in water with 1 teaspoon of shampoo. Rinse until the water runs clear.

6. Squeeze out the wet wool, and roll in a dry towel to remove excess water. Hang the wool to dry.

7. Overdye with indigo to create greens, and overdye with any of the reds (cochineal, lac, or madder to name a few) to create orange shades. Use an iron mordant, and the color should turn to olive green.

68
Yarrow

(Achillea millefolium)

- Very good lightfastness
- 4 cups of flowers
- Mordant used: For a $1/2$-yard of wool, 1 teaspoon of alum and a $1/2$-teaspoon of cream of tartar
- Yellow shades

Yarrow is a perennial herb that grows in the United States, Europe, and Asia. Yellow, white, or pink flowers blossom from June through September, and these blooms are the source of your dye. The flowers can be used either fresh or dried.

The Recipe:

1. Use a $1/2$-yard of wet wool. (An alum mordant should be applied beforehand.)

2. To extract the dye from the flowers, soak 4 cups in a mesh bag in water overnight.

3. Add water to this solution to fill a large pot and heat just to a simmer for 1 hour.

4. Add the wet wool and simmer for 1 hour. Turn off the heat.

5. Let the wool cool in the pot overnight.

6. Remove the wool, and wash in water with 1 teaspoon of shampoo. Rinse until the water runs clear.

7. Squeeze out the wet wool, and roll in a dry towel to remove excess water. Hang the wool to dry.

8. Overdye with indigo to create greens, and overdye with any of the reds (cochineal, lac, or madder to name a few) to create orange shades. Add an iron mordant and an olive green color will occur.

69
Yellow Cosmos

(Cosmos sulphureus)

- Fair lightfastness
- 4 cups of flowers
- Mordant used: For a $1/2$-yard of wool, 1 teaspoon of alum and a $1/2$-teaspoon of cream of tartar
- Yellow shades

Cosmos is an annual flower that can grow up to 4 feet tall. The yellow flowers you'll want to use for the dye are in bloom all summer long. The flowers can be used either fresh or dried.

The Recipe:

1. Use a $1/2$-yard of wet wool. (An alum mordant should be applied beforehand.)

2. To extract the dye from the flowers, soak 4 cups in a mesh bag in water overnight.

3. Add water to this solution to fill a large pot and heat just to a simmer for 1 hour.

4. Add the wet wool and simmer for 1 hour. Turn off the heat.

5. Let the wool cool in the pot overnight.

6. Remove the wool, and wash in water with 1 teaspoon of shampoo. Rinse until the water runs clear.

7. Squeeze out the wet wool, and roll in a dry towel to remove excess water. Hang the wool to dry.

8. Overdye with indigo to create greens, and overdye with any of the reds (cochineal, lac, or madder to name a few) to create orange shades.

70
Zinnia

(Zinnia)

- Fair lightfastness
- 4 cups of flowers
- Mordant used: For a $1/2$-yard of wool,
  1 teaspoon of alum and a $1/2$-teaspoon of cream
  of tartar
- Yellow shades

Zinnias are annual flowers that produce a variety of colored blossoms. They bloom throughout the summer and into the fall. The flowers are used for the dye.

The Recipe:

1. Use a $1/2$-yard of wet wool. (An alum mordant should be applied beforehand.)

2. To extract the dye from the flowers, soak 4 cups in a mesh bag in water overnight.

3. Add water to this solution to fill a large pot and heat just to a simmer for 1 hour.

4. Add the wet wool and simmer for 1 hour. Turn off the heat.

5. Let the wool cool in the pot overnight.

6. Remove the wool, and wash in water with 1 teaspoon of shampoo. Rinse until the water runs clear.

7. Squeeze out the wet wool, and roll in a dry towel to remove excess water. Hang the wool to dry.

8. Overdye with indigo to create greens, and overdye with any of the reds (cochineal, lac, or madder to name a few) to create orange shades.

A Gallery of Naturally Dyed Rugs

Bringing Colors to Life in Wool

RIGHT FROM THE BEGINNING OF MY RUG HOOKING "CAREER," I found it exciting and satisfying to grow dye plants in my garden, harvest them into glorious dye colors, and hook them into a finished rug. The labor of love involved with transforming plants into colorful wool makes my rugs more personal and individual. Since there are endless combinations of dyes that produce a variety of colors, I feel like this pursuit is an ongoing subject.

Now that I have shared the process and recipes of natural dyeing, I felt it was only fitting to allow you to see the finished result—the rugs themselves. After all, what better way is there to appreciate the fruits of your labor than viewing the finished rugs, hooked elaborately with a myriad of beautiful, naturally dyed colors?

All of the rugs shown here have wool that has been dyed naturally. Unfortunately, I used such a variety and mixture of naturally dyed wool that I couldn't even begin to unravel each rug and tell you which rug was dyed with which colors! These rugs, however, will give you an idea of the kind of amazing results you can achieve using wool dyed with natural sources.

I especially enjoyed using indigo-dyed wool in my pieces. Knowing that only a few plants produce a blue color makes the wool even more special to hook with. I also love the many different shades of green I can produce when I overdye the indigo with yellows. When hooking a landscape, these greens just seem to blend in perfectly.

In closing, I hope this book will entice rug hookers and other fiber artists to use natural dyes in their art. By passing on the unique techniques of natural dyeing, I feel that I am preserving a valuable part of the heritage of this ancient craft. And I truly believe that natural dyeing is an aspect of the fiber arts that needs to be preserved and treasured.

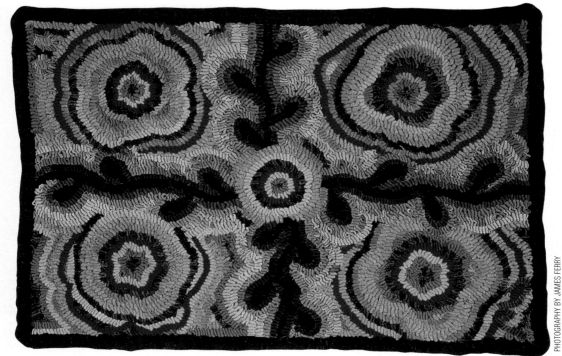

Pink Flowers, 28" x 19", hand-torn wool on linen. Designed and hooked by Marie Sugar, Ellicott City, Maryland, 2000.

Fan Rug, 34" x 24", #8-cut wool on linen. Designed and hooked by Marie Sugar, Ellicott City, Maryland, 1999.

Welcome Star, 28" x 28", #8-cut wool on linen. Designed and hooked by Marie Sugar, Ellicott City, Maryland, 1999.

Leaf, 19" x 22", #8-cut wool on linen. Designed and hooked by Marie Sugar, Ellicott City, Maryland, 1999. A hooked and penny rug.

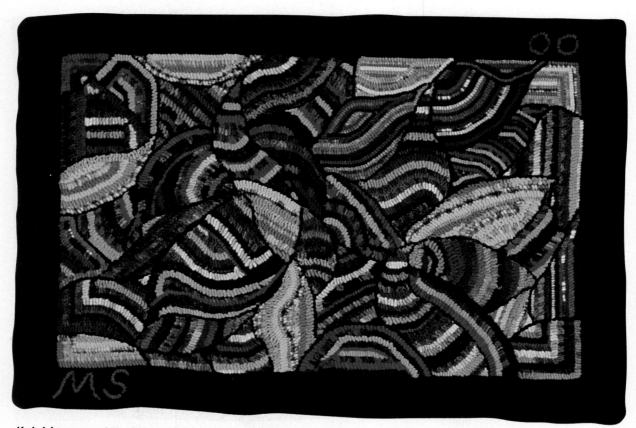

Kaleidoscope, 36" x 24", hand-torn wool on linen. Designed and hooked by Marie Sugar, Ellicott City, Maryland, 2000.

Black Dog, 22" x 19", #8-cut wool on linen. Designed and hooked by Marie Sugar, Ellicott City, Maryland, 1999. A hooked and penny rug.

Flowers in a Pot, 22" x 19", #8-cut wool on linen. Designed and hooked by Marie Sugar, Ellicott City, Maryland, 1999. A hooked and penny rug.

Rooster, 19" x 22", #8-cut wool on linen. Designed and hooked by Marie Sugar, Ellicott City, Maryland, 1999,

The Crow, 14" x 21", #6-cut wool on linen. Designed and hooked by Marie Sugar, Ellicott City, Maryland, 1998.

Home, 18" x 18", #6-cut wool on linen. Designed and hooked by Marie Sugar, Ellicott City, Maryland, 1999.

Six Sided Star, 29" x 22", #8-cut wool on linen. Designed and hooked by Marie Sugar, Ellicott City, Maryland, 1999.

Cottage Rose, 22" x 29", #8-cut wool on linen. Designed and hooked by Marie Sugar, Ellicott City, Maryland, 1999.

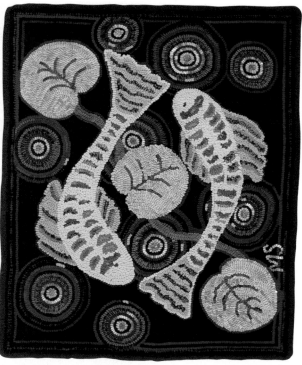

Fish Pond, 22" x 28", #8-cut wool on linen. Designed and hooked by Marie Sugar, Ellicott City, Maryland, 2000.

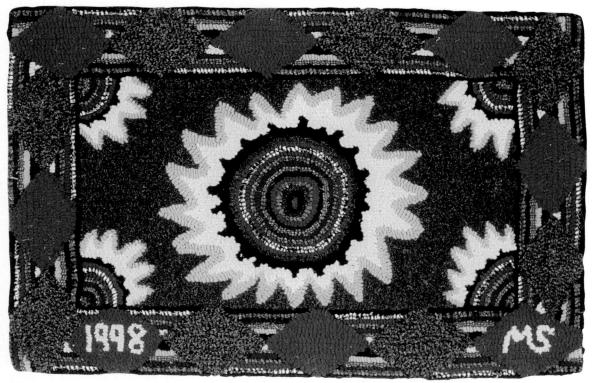

Nova, 21" x 14", #6-cut wool on linen. Designed and hooked by Marie Sugar, Ellicott City, Maryland, 1998.

Two Moons, 35" x 23", #6-cut wool on linen. Designed and hooked by Marie Sugar, Ellicott City, Maryland, 1999.

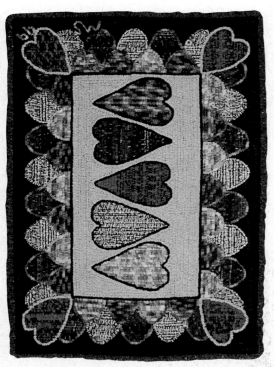

Two Grey Cats, 21" x 28", #8-cut wool on linen. Designed and hooked by Marie Sugar, Ellicott City, Maryland, 1999.

Hearts, 24" x 34", #8-cut wool on linen. Designed and hooked by Marie Sugar, Ellicott City, Maryland, 1999.

Leaf and Log Cabin, 29" x 19", #8-cut wool on linen. Designed and hooked by Marie Sugar, Ellicott City, Maryland, 1999.

Red Pot of Flowers, 24" x 16", #6-cut wool on linen. Designed and hooked by Marie Sugar, Ellicott City, Maryland, 1998.

The Dyes-by-Color Index

Mail-Order Suppliers

EARTH GUILD, INC.
33 Haywood Street
Asheville, NC 28801
Phone: (800) 327-8448
E-mail: *inform@earthguild.com*

**EARTHUES,
A NATURAL COLOR
COMPANY**
5129 Ballard Avenue N.W.
Seattle, WA 98107
Phone: (206) 789-1065
E-mail: *earthues@aol.com*

**FLINTRIDGE WOODSHOP
& FIBERS**
121 Woodcrest Road
Sister Bay, WI 54234
Phone: (920) 854-2919
E-mail: *gjischke@itol.com*

**HANGIN' ROUND DYE
SPOONS**
Connie Bradley
18550 Pitts Road
Wellington, OH 44090
Phone: (440) 647-2473
E-mail: *osurug@ix.netcom.com*

MARYANNE LINCOLN
10 Oak Point
Wrentham, MA 01093
Phone: (508) 384-8188

MANNINGS
1132 Green Ridge Road
PO Box 687
East Berlin, PA 17316
Phone: (717) 624-2223
E-mail: *mannings@sun-link.com*
Website: *http://www.the-mannings.com*

PRO CHEMICAL & DYE
PO Box 14
Somerset, MA 02726
Phone: (888) 2-BUY-DYE (228-9393)
Fax: (508) 676-3980
Technical Support: (508) 676-3838
Website: *www.prochemical.com*

RUMPELSTILTSKIN
1021 R Street
Sacramento. CA 95814
Phone: (916) 442-9225

**THE TRIPLE OVER DYE
FAMILY**
Janet Matthews
187 Jane Drive
Syracuse, NY 13219
Phone: (315) 468-2616

WALNUT RIDGE FARM
Bill and Judy Mackenroth
153 Marwood Road
Cabot, PA 16023
Phone: (724) 352-4025

W. CUSHING COMPANY
21 North Street, PO Box 351
Kennebunkport, ME 04046
Phone: (800) 626-7847
E-mail: *customer@w.cushing.com*
Website: *www.wcushing.com*

Bibliography

■ Adrosko, Rita
Natural Dyes and Home Dyeing
New York: Dover Publications, Inc., 1971

■ Brooklyn Botanic Garden
Dye Plants and Dyeing
New York: Brooklyn Botanic Gardens, 1971

■ Brooklyn Botanic Garden
Natural Plant Dyeing
New York: Brooklyn Botanic Gardens, 1976

■ Brown, Rachel
The Weaving, Spinning, and Dyeing Book
New York: Alfred A Knopf, 1998

■ Buchanan, Rita
A Dyer's Garden
Colorado, USA: Interweave Press, Inc., 1995

■ Casselman, Karen Leigh
Craft of the Dyer
New York: Dover Publications, Inc., 1993

■ Davidson, Mary Frances
The Dye-Pot
Tennessee, USA: Mary Frances Davidson, 1997

■ Dean, Jenny
Wild Color
New York: Watson-Guptell Publications, 1999

■ Dean, Jenny
The Craft of Natural Dyeing
Great Britain: Search Press, Ltd., 1994

■ Liles, J.N.
The Art and Craft of Natural Dyeing
New York: University of Tennessee Press, 1990

■ McRae, Bobbi
Colors from Nature
Vermont, USA: A Storey Publishing Book, 1993

■ Robertson, Seonaid
Dyes from Plants
New York: Van Nostrand Reinhold Co., 1973

Glossary

A

ACORN: A nut from the oak tree that produces tan and brown shades.

ADJECTIVE: A dye that requires a mordant to affix the color to the fiber.

ALKANET: A member of the borage family. The plant grows in Europe and Great Britain. The dried roots produce a purple or brown dye.

ALUM: Aluminum potassium sulfate. A mordant used in the dyeing process.

AMMONIA: An assistant.

ANILINE: A coal tar used in the invention of synthetic dyes.

ANNATTO: A shrub native to South and Central America. The reddish-orange dye is obtained from the seeds.

ASSISTANT: Used in the dyeing process to alter the color of the dye.

ASTER: Both an annual and a perennial plant. The fresh flowers are used to make a yellow dye.

B

BACHELOR'S BUTTON: A yellow dye comes from this perennial plant. It has blue flowers and grows to 2 feet tall.

BAKING SODA: An assistant used to alter color.

BARBERRY: An ornamental shrub. The berries produce a yellow dye.

BEDSTRAW: Also called lady's bedstraw. The flowers produce pink shades.

BEET: A fugitive dye that produces pink shades.

BEGONIA: A flowering bulb. A wide variety of dye shades are possible depending on the color of flowers dyed with.

BIRCH: An ornamental tree. The white, paper-like bark produces yellow shades of dye.

BLACK-EYED SUSAN: A perennial also known as coneflower. Yellow shades are obtained from the flowers.

BLACK WALNUT: Tree native to North America. The hulls are used and produce brown shades.

BLUE VITRIOL: Also known as copper, this is a mordant used in the dyeing process.

BRAZILWOOD: The rose shades are produced from the wood chips of certain redwood trees.

BURDOCK: A biennial weed. The leaves produce yellow shades.

BUTTERNUT: Beige shades are produced from the hulls of this tree.

BLACK DYES: Obtained by overdyeing a number of colors.

C

CACTUS: The cochineal insects feed on cacti.

CARROT: Yellow shades are achieved from using the green tops of carrots.

CHAMOMILE: Used as a food source. The flowers and leaves produce a yellow dye.

CHROME: Bichromate of potash: potassium dichromate. A mordant.

CLEMATIS: Flowering perennial vine. The flowers and vines produce yellow-green shades.

COCHINEAL: Rose and red shades are produced when dyeing with this dried insect native to Mexico and South America.

COFFEE: The grinds dye brown and tan shades.

COPPER: A mordant.

COPPER PENNIES: The copper in the pennies produces grey shades when soaking in a solution of ammonia and water.

COPPER SULFATE: Blue vitriol. A mordant.

COREOPSIS: Either an annual or a perennial, the flowers produce a yellow dye.

CREAM OF TARTAR: Tartaric acid. Used as an assistant and with alum.

CUTCH: A brown dye from the heartwood of the Acacia Catechu native to Burma and India.

D

DAFFODIL: Bulbs that multiply. The flowers produce a yellow dye.

DAHLIA: Bulbs that can grow to five feet. The flowers produce yellow shades.

DAISY: Wildflowers common throughout the United States and Canada. A yellow-green dye comes from the flowers.

DELPHINIUM: Tall perennial with a variety of colored flowers from which yellow shades are produced.

DANDELION: A common weed. Yellow shades are achieved from the yellow flowers.

DYE BATH: The dye material mixed with water.

DYER'S BROOM: Also called dyer's greenweed. The flowers and leaves produce yellow shades. Has a history of use dating back to the 9th century.

E

ELDERBERRY: A shrub with purple berries. Pink shades are obtained from the berries.

F

FASTNESS: A system of rating the fading of dyes from exposure to light.

FERROUS SULFATE IRON: A mordant.

FUGITIVE: Colors that fade over time.

FUSTIC: Also known as old fustic. The yellow-orange dye comes from the heartwood of a tree that is a member of the mulberry family.

G

GERANIUM: A house and garden plant. Light green shades are produced by the flowers and leaves.

GLAUBER'S SALT: Slows down the absorption of dyes in the wool. An assistant.

GOLDENROD: A wildflower found in the United States and Canada. Produces yellow shades from the flowers.

GRASS: A yellow-green dye is obtained from newly mowed grass.

H

HEARTWOOD: The wood chips from which the dye comes.

HENNA: A tree native to India, Egypt, and the Middle East. The yellow-brown shades are also used to dye hair and skin.

HIBISCUS: Also called rose mallow. A maroon dye is obtained from the red flowers.

HOLLYHOCK: A mauve or maroon dye is produced from the red flowers of this plant.

I

INDIGO: Considered a vat dye. A completely different process is used to dye blue shades from this plant.

INSECT: The insect cochineal produces a red dye, and the resin from another insect produces the red dye, lac.

IRIS: The flowers produce a yellow dye. Irises are grown from tubers.

IRON: A mordant. Also known as copperas and ferrous sulfate.

IVY: The leaves produce a yellow-green dye from this evergreen vine.

J

JOE-PYE WEED: A perennial tall wildflower with purple flowers. These flowers produce a yellow dye.

L

LAC: Resin secreted by scale insects living on the ficus tree in India. Mulberry or red dye is produced.

LAMB'S EAR: A perennial plant with leaves that feel like velvet. A yellow dye is produced by the leaves and stalks.

LICHEN: A fungal plant used in dyeing.

LILY: A perennial flower common in the United States. Yellow shades are produced from the flowers.

LOGWOOD: The purple dye comes from the heartwood of a tree that grows in Central and South America and the West Indies.

M

MADDER: A perennial plant native to the Middle East, Europe, and Asia. The red dye it produces is an ancient dye thats use dates back to the 1st century.

MAHONIA: The purple berries produce lavender shades from this evergreen shrub.

MARIGOLD: Annuals common in the United States. The flowers produce the yellow dye.

MINT: Yellow-green shades are produced from the leaves of this perennial plant.

MORDANT: A mineral salt that binds the dye to the fabric and affects its color.

MULLEIN: A tall biennial. Yellow shades are achieved from the leaves and stalks.

MUSHROOMS: A variety of shades can be obtained from certain species of mushrooms.

N

NASTURTIUM: An annual flowering plant. Yellow shades are produced from the flowers.

NETTLE: The stinging nettle is considered a weed. Yellow shades are obtained from the leaves and stalks.

O

ONION: Both red and yellow onion skins can be used to produce yellow, orange, and rust shades. No mordant is necessary.

OSAGE ORANGE: The yellow dye comes from a tree also known as hedge apple. Wood chips contain the dye.

OLD FUSTIC: Another name for fustic.

OVERDYE: To first dye with one color, then to dye over with another color. The process changes the color of the fabric.

P

PANSY: A yellow, beige, or pink dye is obtained from these annual flowers.

PEONY: Perennials with large flowers that produce a yellow dye.

PETUNIA: An annual plant that produces yellow shades.

PLANTAIN: A common weed used as a food source. Produces a yellow-green dye.

POKEBERRY: Considered a weed, it is a perennial shrub producing purple berries from which a red dye is obtained.

POMEGRANATE: The yellow or tan dye comes from the edible fruit on a tree found in Europe, the Middle East, India, the West Indies, and North Africa.

POPPY: Perennial plants with a variety of flower colors producing beige shades.

PREMORDANTING: The process of applying a mordant to fabric before the dyeing process. This is a necessary procedure for some dyes in order for the dye to stick to the fabric.

PRESOAKING: The act of soaking the fabric before applying mordant or dye.

PRIMROSE: Pale yellow shades are produced from a variety of flower colors on this perennial plant.

PURSLANE: Considered a weed, it is used as a food source. The leaves and stems produce yellow shades.

Q

QUEEN ANNE'S LACE: Also called wild carrot. Considered a weed. The flowers produce yellow-green shades.

R

RHODODENDRON: The leaves are used for the yellow dye. It is an evergreen flowering shrub.

RHUBARB: A food source. Yellow-green dye comes from the leaves, and an orange dye comes from the roots

ROCKET, DYER'S: Also known as weld.

RECORD KEEPING: Helpful to keep track of what results were achieved with each dye recipe.

ROOTS: The source of dye from many plants.

ROSE: A flowering shrub. Use the petals to produce shades of yellow.

S

SAFFLOWER: An annual thistle. The fresh or dried flowers produce a yellow dye.

SAGE: An herb. A yellow-green dye is produced from the leaves.

SAINT-JOHN'S-WORT: A perennial plant. The yellow dye comes from the flowers.

SANDALWOOD: A small tree. The dye comes from the heartwood and produces coral and peach shades.

SHASTA DAISY: A pale yellow shade is produced from this perennial plant.

SORREL: A perennial herb. Use the arrowhead-shaped leaves to produce a yellow-green dye.

SQUASH: Use the peels of the squash to produce a yellow dye.

SUBSTANTIVE: A dye that requires no mordants.

SUMAC: A perennial shrub. The purple berries produce tan and brown shades. No mordant is necessary.

SUNFLOWER: A food source. Tall growing annuals. The yellow shades come from the flowers.

T

TANSY: An annual herb. The yellow-green dye comes from the flowers and leaves.

TEA: Black tea is used to produce tan shades. No mordant is necessary.

TIN: Stannous chloride. A mordant.

TOMATO: Use the vines to produce yellow-green shades.

TURMERIC: A member of the ginger family. Bright yellow shades are produced from the tuber of this plant.

TULIP: A flowering bulb with a variety of colored flowers. The flowers produce a yellow dye.

V

VINEGAR: An assistant. Used to alter colors.

W

WASHING SODA: An assistant. Used in vat dyeing.

WELD: Also known as "dyer's rocket." Hardy annual used in Roman times. Bright yellow colors come from the leaves, flowers, and stalks.

WOAD: A source of blue dye. A vat dye.

Y

YARROW: A perennial herb. Grows in the United States, Europe, and Asia. Yellow shades are produced from the flowers.

YELLOW COSMOS: An annual plant. The yellow flowers produce a yellow dye.

YELLOW DOCK: Also called "Curly Dock." A hardy perennial native to Europe and the United States. Yellow shades come from the roots.

Z

ZINNIA: An annual plant that produces a variety of colored flowers. The flowers produce a yellow dye.